GCSE English

Romeo and Juliet

by William Shakespeare

Studying English texts can give you a real headache,
but happily this CGP book makes your life just a little bit easier.

This book has everything you need to write a brilliant essay about *Romeo and Juliet*.
It doesn't just tell you what happens — it's got analysis of the main characters,
themes, historical background and language features too.

Plus, there are plenty of practice questions and a worked exam answer
with tips on how to improve your grade on the big day.

And of course, we've done our best to make the whole
experience at least vaguely entertaining for you.

The Text Guide

CONTENTS

CONTENTS

Published by CGP

Editors:
David Broadbent
Holly Corfield-Carr
Josephine Gibbons
Jennifer Underwood

With thanks to Luke von Kotze and Nicola Woodfin for the proofreading, and
Laura Jakubowski and Laura Stoney for the copyright research.

Acknowledgements
Cover Image: Romeo and Juliet, 1884 (oil on canvas) by Dicksee, Sir Frank (1853-1928)
Southampton City Art Gallery, Hampshire, UK/ The Bridgeman Art Library
Image on page 1: The Reconciliation of the Montagues and the Capulets over the Dead Bodies of Romeo and Juliet (oil
on canvas) by Leighton, Frederic (1830-96) Private Collection/ Photo © Christie's Images/ The Bridgeman Art Library
Images on pages 3, 12, 14, 30, 31 & 32 from the Shakespeare's Globe Theatre production of Romeo & Juliet,
photographer John Haynes
With thanks to iStockphoto.com for permission to use the images on pages 1, 5, 47 & 51
With thanks to Rex Features for permission to use the images on pages 4, 5, 18, 20, 27, 29, 33, 44, & 46
With thanks to The Moviestore Collection for permission to use the images on pages 3, 4, 5, 10, 11, 13, 15, 16, 17, 24,
26, 28, 37, 38, 39, 41, 49 & 53
With thanks to Alamy for permission to use the images on pages 2, 3, 7, 19, 21, 25, 40, 48, 50 & 52
Images on pages 3, 6, 8, 9, 34 & 54 © PARAMOUNT / THE KOBAL COLLECTION

ISBN: 978 1 84146 118 2
Website: www.cgpbooks.co.uk
Printed by Elanders Ltd, Newcastle upon Tyne.
Clipart from CorelDRAW®

Based on the classic CGP style created by Richard Parsons.

Introduction to 'Romeo and Juliet' and Shakespeare

'Romeo and Juliet' is a Tragic Love Story

- *Romeo and Juliet* is about a young couple who fall in <u>love</u> even though their <u>families</u> are <u>enemies</u>.

- This forbidden love leads them to <u>kill</u> themselves, but their deaths bring their families <u>together</u>.

- It's probably the most <u>famous</u> love story in the world, and the plot has been adapted into <u>musicals</u>, <u>operas</u>, and lots of different <u>films</u>.

Romeo and Juliet is about love and hate

1) Shakespeare presents <u>love</u> as an <u>overwhelming force</u> that causes Romeo and Juliet to give up their <u>families</u>, their <u>friends</u> and eventually their <u>lives</u>.

2) The <u>feud</u> between Romeo's and Juliet's families causes a lot of violence and death — Shakespeare shows how <u>pointless</u> and <u>destructive</u> hate is.

Shakespeare is the most Famous writer in the English language

- William Shakespeare wrote at least <u>thirty-seven plays</u> and a lot of <u>poems</u>.

- He wrote some of the most <u>famous</u> plays in the English language, including <u>comedies</u> (such as *Twelfth Night*), <u>tragedies</u> (such as *Macbeth* and *Hamlet*) and <u>histories</u> (such as *Richard III*).

- *Romeo and Juliet* is one of his best-known <u>tragedies</u>.

- It was written in the <u>1580s or 1590s</u>, but the story is based on <u>earlier</u> tragedies.

1564	Born in <u>Stratford-upon-Avon</u>, Warwickshire.
1582	Married <u>Anne Hathaway</u>.
1583-85	Had three children — Susanna, Hamnet and Judith.
1585-92	Began an <u>acting career</u> in <u>London</u>.
1589-1613	Wrote most of his plays.
1597	First printed version of '<u>Romeo and Juliet</u>' published.
1616	Died, aged 52.

Background Information

'Romeo and Juliet' is set in the Italian city of Verona

Here's a plan of the important places in the play, showing where all the important action happens.

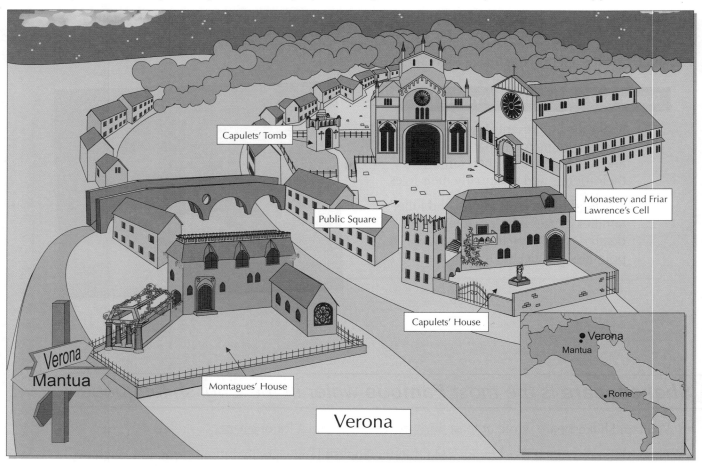

Theatre was an important form of Entertainment

The rebuilt Globe Theatre in London.

- There was no TV, radio or internet in Shakespeare's time, so going to the theatre was really popular.

- The theatre wasn't just for rich people — Shakespeare's audiences included servants and labourers. They could get quite rowdy during performances.

- The poorer people in the audience stood in front of the stage — if it rained, they got wet. The richer people sat in the covered galleries above.

- Shakespeare's theatre company, the King's Men (previously called the Lord Chamberlain's Men), performed in the Globe Theatre in London. This was rebuilt in 1997.

- It was illegal for women to act, so the women's parts were played by young boys (even Juliet...).

Who's Who in 'Romeo and Juliet'

Romeo Montague...

... is a young man who's romantic and passionate. He falls in love with Juliet.

Juliet Capulet...

... is a young girl whose parents want her to marry a man called Paris. She falls in love with Romeo.

The Montagues...

... Romeo's parents, who hate the Capulets.

The Capulets...

... Juliet's parents, who hate the Montagues.

The Friar...

... is an expert on the uses of herbs. He's a father figure to Romeo.

The Nurse...

... has brought Juliet up since she was a baby. They're very close.

Mercutio...

... is Romeo's friend. He's a joker and doesn't take life too seriously.

Tybalt...

... is Juliet's cousin. He hates the Montagues and is always starting fights.

Benvolio...

... is Romeo's cousin and best friend. He's usually quite peaceful.

Paris...

... is a rich young man who wants to marry Juliet.

'Romeo and Juliet' — Plot Summary

'Romeo and Juliet'... what happens when?

Romeo and Juliet needs to be as familiar to you as your favourite socks. This little recap of the <u>main events</u> will help you on your way, but it's no substitute for reading the play. There's no escaping that I'm afraid...

Act One — A *Fight* and a *Fancy-Dress Ball*

- There's a <u>fight</u> between two <u>rival families</u>, the <u>Montagues</u> and the <u>Capulets</u>. The Prince stops the fighting.

- <u>Romeo</u> tells his friend Benvolio that he's unhappy because Rosaline <u>doesn't love</u> him.

- <u>Paris</u> asks Capulet if he can <u>marry</u> his daughter <u>Juliet</u>. Capulet says he'll think about it. The Capulets throw a <u>ball</u>.

- Mercutio is invited to the ball, but Romeo and Benvolio <u>gate-crash</u>.

- Romeo and Juliet <u>meet</u> for the first time. They <u>talk</u> and <u>kiss</u> without realising that their families are <u>enemies</u> — but they find out afterwards.

Act Two — *Romeo* and *Juliet* get *Married* in *Secret*

- Romeo sneaks into the Capulets' garden to look for Juliet. Juliet is at her <u>window</u>, thinking out loud about how much she likes Romeo. Romeo <u>overhears</u>, and then comes to talk to her. They decide to get <u>married</u>.

- Romeo goes to <u>Friar Lawrence</u> and asks him for help. The Friar agrees to marry Romeo and Juliet.

- Romeo meets his friends, Mercutio and Benvolio, and they <u>tease</u> the Nurse as she gives Romeo a <u>message</u> from Juliet.

- The Nurse tells Juliet that the <u>wedding</u> has been organised for that afternoon.

- Romeo and Juliet get <u>married</u> in <u>secret</u>.

Acts Three and Four — Two real **Deaths** and a **Fake** one

- Juliet's cousin Tybalt <u>kills Mercutio</u> in a fight. Romeo <u>kills Tybalt</u> in revenge. The Prince <u>banishes</u> Romeo from Verona as punishment.

- Romeo and Juliet spend the night <u>together</u>, then Romeo <u>leaves</u> the city.

- Juliet's parents tell her that she's going to <u>marry Paris</u> in two days' time, whether she likes it or not. She <u>can't</u>, because she's <u>already married</u> to Romeo.

- Juliet asks the <u>Friar</u> for help. He has a <u>plan</u>.

- Juliet <u>fakes</u> her own <u>death</u> with a sleeping potion. Friar Lawrence sends Romeo a letter telling him to <u>rescue</u> her from the tomb when the potion wears off.

- Juliet's family think that she's <u>dead</u> and <u>bury</u> her in the family tomb.

Act Five — It's not a **Happy Ending**

- Romeo <u>doesn't get</u> the Friar's <u>letter</u> — he hears that Juliet is <u>dead</u>, and goes to her tomb to <u>kill himself</u>.

- Paris sees Romeo going into the tomb. They <u>fight</u>, and Romeo <u>kills</u> Paris.

- Romeo lies next to Juliet and <u>drinks poison</u>.

- Friar Lawrence finds out that Romeo didn't get the letter, so he goes to the tomb and arrives just as <u>Juliet wakes up</u>.

- The Friar doesn't want to get into <u>trouble</u> for Romeo's death. When Juliet won't come away from the tomb with him, he <u>runs away</u>.

- Juliet is left <u>alone</u>. When she realises that Romeo is dead she <u>kills herself</u>.

- Everyone arrives at the tomb. The Friar is brought back by a watchman and <u>explains</u> what has happened.

- Montague and Capulet realise that their <u>feud</u> caused the <u>death</u> of their children. They make <u>peace</u>.

Double suicide — so much for a happy ending...

Once you're confident that you know what happens in *Romeo and Juliet*, you're ready to start Section One. If you're still not sure about the plot or want a break from revision, have a look at the *Romeo and Juliet* cartoon at the back of the book.

How Plays Work

Lots of people think Shakespeare's the hardest thing you have to study for English —
and they're right... but it should be less hard and less weird when you've read this section.

'Romeo and Juliet' is meant to be Watched — Not Read

1) *Romeo and Juliet* is a <u>play</u>. A play tells a story by <u>showing</u> it to you.

2) When you <u>read</u> the play, it's often pretty hard to <u>follow</u> what's going on.
   Try to <u>imagine</u> what's happening, how the people would <u>speak</u> and <u>act</u> —
   it should all start to make a lot more sense.

3) If you can, try to see the play <u>on stage</u>. If not, watch a <u>film</u> version to get an idea of the <u>story</u>.

4) But remember to <u>read the play</u> as well — films often <u>cut scenes</u> and <u>change</u> the language, so it's
   <u>dangerous</u> to rely on them too much.

Romeo and Juliet is a Tragedy

Romeo and Juliet is one of Shakespeare's <u>most famous</u> tragedies. Mostly, it's a <u>typical tragedy</u>...

1) It's about some <u>serious topics</u> like <u>love</u> and <u>death</u>.

2) It's <u>sad</u> and <u>moving</u>.

3) The main characters <u>die</u> at the end.

But there are also a few <u>less tragic</u> things...

4) There's some saucy comedy <u>banter</u>
   between <u>Romeo</u> and his <u>friends</u>.

5) Juliet's <u>Nurse</u> is a fairly <u>comic character</u> —
   always flustered and over-the-top.

6) Some scenes between Romeo and Juliet are <u>romantic</u> and <u>optimistic</u>.

Pay Attention to the Stage Directions

When you're reading the play, look at the <u>stage directions</u> — they're little phrases in italics that
tell the actors <u>what</u> to do, <u>when</u> to come in and when to <u>leave</u> the stage.

These are the really <u>common</u> stage directions in <u>Shakespeare</u>:

Enter	=	when someone <u>comes onto</u> the stage
Exit	=	when one person <u>leaves</u> the stage
Exeunt	=	when <u>more</u> than one person <u>leaves</u>
Aside	=	the character is <u>talking</u> to <u>themselves</u>, not to other characters on the stage

Tragedy — when the feeling's gone and you can't go on...

Romeo and Juliet's not just your average tragedy like the other big ones (*Macbeth, Hamlet,* etc). It's not all doom,
gloom, revenge, death — there's love, optimism and funny bits too. Don't forget that when you're writing an essay —
otherwise it might look like you skipped straight to the violent and gory bits instead of reading the whole play.

How to Understand Shakespeare's Language

Shakespeare's plays can be more confusing than a fox and ferret convention, especially all the strange ye olde language. But there are certain ways of reading it so it makes more sense...

The **Play** is written in **Poetry** and **Prose**

1) Some of the play is written in poetry — but the poetry doesn't always rhyme.

2) The poetry is the bits where all the lines are roughly the same length, and each line starts with a capital letter. It looks like this:

> "Is there no pity sitting in the clouds
> That sees into the bottom of my grief?
> O sweet my mother, cast me not away!"
> Act 3, Scene 5

3) Some bits of the play are in prose — prose is normal sentences without any set rhythm.

4) Common characters, like the Nurse and the servants, usually speak in prose.

For more on poetry see Section 4.

5) Any bits of comedy in the play are in prose — even if it's the main characters speaking.

Don't Stop Reading at the End of Each Line

1) Even though each line starts with a capital letter, it doesn't mean it's a separate sentence.

2) Just ignore the capitals and follow the punctuation.

3) For example, there's no full stop here so carry on to the next line:

> "And, to say truth, Verona brags of him
> To be a virtuous and well-governed youth"
> Act 1, Scene 5

© Moviestore collection Ltd / Alamy

Look Out for Words in a Funny Order

1) Another reason Shakespeare can be tricky to understand is the long complicated sentences.

2) It's hard because the words are in a funny order. If you change the order it makes it easier to understand. For example:

> "A glooming peace this morning with it brings"
> Act 5, Scene 3

> This morning brings a glooming peace with it.

> "Sweet flower, with flowers thy bridal bed I strew"
> Act 5, Scene 3

> Sweet flower, I strew thy bridal bed with flowers.

How to Read Shakespeare's Language

Romeo and Juliet is full of cobwebby, dusty old words — and weird ways of writing things using apostrophes. Don't let them put you off — it is English really. I promise.

You have to **Guess** what the **Missing Letters are**

1) Shakespeare often <u>runs two words together</u> and misses letters out to make them fit into a line.

2) There's often an <u>apostrophe</u> instead of the <u>missing letter</u>. So "to't" means "to it".

> **Act 3, Scene 5**
>
> Trust to't, bethink you, I'll not be forsworn.

3) If you come across random apostrophes when you're reading, you'll have to <u>work out</u> what the missing letters are.

© PARAMOUNT / THE KOBAL COLLECTION

Mind Your **Thees**, **Thous** and **Thys**

1) They had <u>different words</u> for 'you' in those days.

2) People used to say '<u>thou</u>' to be familiar or friendly, and '<u>you</u>' to be more formal. Look out for these words:

Thou	=	You	Thine	=	Your
Thee	=	You	Thy	=	Your

And finally, some more **Old**, **Confusing Words**

1) <u>Verbs</u> often look a bit <u>different</u> from modern English...

wert thou	=	were you	thou wilt	=	you will
thou hast	=	you have	thou swear'st	=	you swear

2) If this seems difficult, here's a trick — <u>take the 't' off</u> the end of the <u>verb</u>:

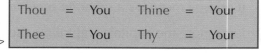

hast – t = has
wilt – t = wil(l)

3) And here are a few more words to watch out for:

hie	=	go (hurry)	wherefore	= why
hither	=	to here	thence	= from <u>there</u>
whence	=	from <u>where</u>	ere	= before
hence	=	from <u>here</u>		

For words funny order in a look out...

Right, so Shakespeare put his words in a funny order. It's very annoying and makes the plays difficult to read. But don't be too mad at him — he didn't start the trend. No. If you go back further into history — in fact, you need to look to a long time ago, in a galaxy far, far away for this — then find someone else you will, hmmm. May the Force be with you.

Analysis of Act One — The Tragedy Begins

This section gives you an analysis of the play, act by act. If you learn all this stuff you'll be on to a winner.

Prologue — The *Whole Story* in Fourteen Lines

See p.41 for more about fate.

1) The <u>prologue</u> tells you the <u>two main points</u> of the play:

   - There's a <u>feud</u> between the Montague and Capulet families.
   - The story's about <u>two lovers</u>, one from <u>each family</u>. They will both <u>die</u>, but their deaths will bring an end to the quarrel.

Theme — Fate

The prologue says Romeo and Juliet are "<u>star-cross'd</u> lovers" — we know from the beginning that they're <u>doomed</u>.

2) Shakespeare introduces the main <u>themes</u> in the prologue — <u>love</u>, <u>death</u>, <u>fate</u>, <u>family</u>, <u>honour</u>, and <u>conflict</u>.

3) This <u>sets the mood</u> for the rest of the play — the audience are expecting <u>drama</u>, <u>tragedy</u>, and lots of fights.

4) The prologue is in the form of a <u>sonnet</u>. It's a <u>summary</u> of the whole play.

Scene One starts Violently

1) The <u>first scene</u> is a <u>sword fight</u> between Montagues and Capulets — it's dramatic and it shows the <u>strength</u> of the <u>violent conflict</u> between the two families.

2) The Prince says that the next person to cause trouble will be <u>executed</u> — this introduces a threat of <u>violence</u>.

3) This is the first scene with <u>Tybalt</u> in — you can see he's going to be <u>trouble</u>. He always wants to <u>fight</u>.

© PARAMOUNT / THE KOBAL COLLECTION

Theme — Conflict

<u>Starting</u> the play with <u>physical violence</u> makes the audience aware that <u>more</u> fighting could happen. The next fight is in Act 3, Scene 1 and it's even <u>worse</u> — people <u>die</u>.

There's Romance in Scenes One, Two and Three

1) In Scene One Romeo's upset because he's <u>in love</u> with <u>Rosaline</u>, who <u>doesn't love him</u>.

2) This shows that Romeo is <u>romantic</u> and <u>emotional</u>. Romeo says that love's <u>confusing</u> — "a <u>choking gall</u>" ("gall" means "bitter") and a "<u>preserving sweet</u>".

3) In Scenes Two and Three, <u>Paris</u> asks Capulet if he can <u>marry Juliet</u>, and her parents want her to think about it.

4) These scenes hint that Romeo and Juliet may <u>become lovers</u> — both of them have some <u>experience</u> of <u>romance</u>, but they're either <u>unhappy</u> or <u>unenthusiastic</u> about it.

5) The characters of <u>Rosaline</u> and <u>Paris</u> make Romeo and Juliet seem even more <u>passionate</u> and <u>loving</u> in <u>contrast</u>.

6) Rosaline is "<u>chaste</u>" (pure) — her character contrasts with Juliet's <u>passionate</u> behaviour later on. Paris is <u>polite</u>, which contrasts with Romeo's <u>inappropriate kissing</u> in Act 1, Scene 5.

Theme — Love

Juliet's relationship with Paris shows a <u>different side</u> to love — it's for <u>financial</u> reasons, as she'll "<u>share</u> all that he doth <u>possess</u>".

So why didn't he just stop after the prologue then...

Ooooh — it's all so dramatic and emotional. Violence, love, dreams and doom... the play really starts with a bang. The prologue is also handy for revision in under a minute. Read that and you know it all. Honest. Okay I'm lying...

Analysis of Act One — Love at First Sight

It's no good rushing this section. In fact that's a terrible idea. It's all too easy to forget what went on *before* all the 'trouble' with Romeo. You get quite a different picture of old Capulet, for starters.

Scene Four — There's a **Ball** at the Capulets' house

© Moviestore Collection Ltd

1) Capulet's having a <u>fancy-dress ball</u>. Romeo and Benvolio <u>shouldn't</u> go to a <u>Capulet</u> party because they're <u>Montagues</u>. This creates <u>suspense</u> — the audience can see it's a <u>bad idea</u>.

2) The tension increases when Romeo says he's had a <u>dream</u> that makes him <u>afraid</u> to go to the party.

Writer's Technique — Foreshadowing
Here, Shakespeare is using <u>foreshadowing</u> — hinting about a <u>future event</u> to the audience. Romeo's <u>worries</u> about the party foreshadow that something <u>bad</u> will happen.

3) Mercutio makes a <u>speech</u> about <u>Queen Mab</u>, who brings dreams to sleepers. This gives the scene a <u>spooky</u> <u>atmosphere</u> because the <u>imagery</u> is mystical.

4) Romeo believes that his <u>dream</u> was <u>warning</u> him about his <u>fate</u>. But Mercutio says that we are <u>responsible</u> for our <u>own dreams</u> — lovers "<u>dream</u> of <u>love</u>".

Theme — Fate
There are lots of times in the play where Romeo gets warnings of terrible events through <u>dreams</u> or <u>visions</u>. This is the first.

Scene Five — **Romance**, but **Trouble's** lurking in the **Background...**

1) Romeo <u>sees Juliet</u> for the first time, but Tybalt spots Romeo, and wants to <u>fight</u> him. Capulet tells Tybalt not to fight at the party, but it highlights how <u>doomed</u> the relationship is.

Theme — Conflict
The <u>hatred</u> of the feud starts to tear them <u>apart</u> from the <u>first time</u> they meet. <u>Tybalt</u> is already threatening violence and they worry about their conflicting <u>family loyalties</u>.

2) Romeo talks to Juliet. Their first conversation is a <u>sonnet</u> — a very <u>structured</u>, <u>traditional love poem</u>.

3) Shakespeare uses the sonnet form to show how well Romeo and Juliet <u>understand each other</u>. Their language slots perfectly together and they immediately <u>match</u> each other's rhymes and rhythms.

Turning Point in the action
Romeo and Juliet fall in love.

Theme — Love
Only <u>three</u> scenes ago Romeo said he was in love with <u>Rosaline</u>, so it's not clear how <u>real</u> his love is for Juliet.

4) Shakespeare uses <u>religious imagery</u> to show that they already <u>worship</u> each other (for more on imagery see p.52-54).

5) But the scene ends in <u>suspense</u> — they find out that their families hate each other — "My <u>only love</u> sprung from my <u>only hate</u>". It seems impossible for them to be together, and the audience is left <u>wondering</u> how they will <u>react</u>.

It's paaarty time...
That party has a lot to answer for — and Romeo shouldn't have even been there in the first place. See — nothing good ever comes from gate-crashing. Except for meeting the love of your life. But she'll probably only die, so is it worth it?

Analysis of Act Two — The 'Balcony' Scene

You've met all the main characters and it's time for the story to really take off. This act has that famous 'balcony' scene — but Shakespeare doesn't actually mention a balcony. Most productions set it on a balcony though.

Prologue and Scene One — Time for a *Recap*

1) Act Two begins with another <u>prologue</u> — a <u>sonnet</u> recaps the story so far.

2) This scene is <u>short</u> — Mercutio and Benvolio look for Romeo, but can't find him so go home.

3) This scene gives the audience a bit of a <u>break</u> from the <u>intense emotional atmospheres</u> of the scenes before and after. It's really just an excuse for some rude jokes about <u>sex</u>.

> **Theme — Love**
>
> Mercutio's comments about "Rosaline's <u>bright eyes</u>" and her "<u>quivering thigh</u>" contrast with Romeo's <u>romantic</u> attitude, but also remind you that <u>desire</u> and passion are important in the play.

Scene Two is the *Famous 'Balcony'* bit

Key Scene

1) This scene's <u>tense</u> and <u>rushed</u>. Romeo and Juliet could get caught <u>at any minute</u>.

2) But there are also <u>intimate</u>, <u>romantic</u> moments. It's the only scene where they're <u>alone</u> for long.

See p.50 for more on soliloquies.

> **Writer's Technique — Soliloquy**
>
> Juliet's speech is a soliloquy. She's <u>talking to herself</u>, but Romeo <u>overhears</u> her — she <u>doesn't know</u> he's beneath her window. Shakespeare does this because it allows Juliet to speak <u>openly</u> about her true feelings for Romeo.

3) Juliet's <u>embarrassed</u> because Romeo's heard her say how much she loves him, but she won't take it back because it's <u>true</u>. This shows that she's <u>modest</u> but also <u>honest</u>.

4) The Nurse is calling her, so Juliet goes inside and comes out again <u>several times</u>, which adds to the <u>rushed feel</u> and shows that it's <u>difficult</u> for them to be <u>alone</u>.

5) The <u>feud</u> means it's <u>dangerous</u> for Romeo to be in the Capulets' garden — everything has to be <u>rushed</u> and <u>secret</u>. Juliet's saying that Romeo should "<u>refuse thy name</u>" and stop being a Montague, or she should stop being a Capulet. That way they could be <u>together</u>.

© Moviestore Collection Ltd

6) Juliet suggests they get <u>married</u>. Romeo promises to organise it by the next day. This <u>rush</u> to get married shows that Juliet is <u>impulsive</u> and <u>romantic</u> — just like Romeo.

> **Theme — Love**
>
> At the <u>beginning</u> of the scene, they have <u>different ideas</u> on love. Romeo <u>worships</u> Juliet and calls her a "<u>bright angel</u>". But Juliet wants something more <u>real</u> and moves the relationship towards <u>marriage</u>.

Whaddya mean there's no balcony...

This is a pretty important part of the play — Romeo and Juliet are so much in love that they're prepared to go against their families. They know what they're doing is dangerous, but they love each other so much they'll risk it — aw...

Analysis of Act Two — Romeo Organises the Wedding

The cat's out of the bag. Romeo loves Juliet, and Juliet loves Romeo. We all know it's going to end in tears, so if I were you I'd enjoy the happy bits while they last. And learn the story.

Scene Three — Romeo Books the Church

1) This is the first scene with the <u>Friar</u>. Romeo explains that he's <u>forgotten</u> Rosaline and wants to <u>marry Juliet</u>.

2) The Friar's <u>amazed</u> that Romeo's in love again, but <u>reluctantly</u> agrees to marry them.

3) The Friar seems like a <u>kind</u>, <u>wise</u> man. He calls Romeo "<u>Young son</u>" and "<u>pupil mine</u>", which suggests that they have a <u>close relationship</u>.

4) But he <u>only</u> agrees to help because it'll turn the feud's "<u>rancour</u> to <u>pure love</u>" — he <u>doesn't believe</u> that Romeo and Juliet are <u>truly in love</u>.

5) The Friar <u>foreshadows</u> quite a few <u>future events</u> in this scene:

- The Friar says that plants used to cure can be misused to kill, as "<u>Virtue</u> itself turns <u>vice</u>". This foreshadows Romeo's suicide by <u>poison</u>, and Juliet's use of a <u>potion</u> to fake her own death.

- He says Romeo has <u>buried</u> his love for Rosaline "in a <u>grave</u>" — which is very close to what happens to Romeo's new love, <u>Juliet</u>.

- The Friar warns Romeo not to rush into things — "they <u>stumble</u> that run <u>fast</u>" — this hints that Romeo's <u>impulsive nature</u> will get him into <u>trouble</u>.

Writer's Technique — Foreshadowing

Shakespeare uses <u>foreshadowing</u> to make the Friar seem <u>very wise</u> — or <u>spookily knowledgeable</u>.

Scene Four — The Nurse Takes a Bit of Stick

1) There's some basic <u>plot progression</u> in this scene — the audience learns that Tybalt has sent a <u>challenge</u> to Romeo, and Romeo passes a message to Juliet (via the Nurse) telling her that the <u>wedding</u> has been <u>arranged</u>.

© John Haynes

2) These two pieces of information signal <u>trouble</u> to the <u>audience</u>. Obviously if Romeo is <u>married</u> to Tybalt's cousin, he won't want to <u>fight</u> him. But as in Act 1, Scene 1, Tybalt can <u>provoke</u> people to fight even if they <u>don't want to</u>.

3) But it's also a <u>light</u>, <u>comic</u> scene which shows us a <u>different side</u> to Romeo. He <u>fools around</u> with Mercutio and Benvolio, and they <u>tease</u> the Nurse.

4) This is the first time Romeo's friends have seen him <u>cheerful</u> since the beginning of the play — Mercutio says "Now art thou <u>sociable</u>, now art thou <u>Romeo</u>". This shows that Juliet has a <u>positive effect</u> on Romeo — she's made him <u>happy</u> and <u>lively</u> again.

Romeo and Juliet — together 'till death us do part'...

... so not that long then. Friar Lawrence is shocked by Romeo's fickle nature — in one evening Romeo's forgotten all about Rosaline and wants to marry Juliet. The Friar isn't sure Romeo is in love, but he sees a chance to end the feud.

Analysis of Act Two — Juliet Waits for News

Two more scenes to go in this act, so make sure you get 'em read and remembered. The clearer you've got the play in your head, the easier it'll be to write about it.

Scene Five — *Good News* for Juliet

1) Juliet waits for the Nurse. Her speech shows the <u>frustration</u> she feels — she can't believe that it's "<u>three hours long</u>, yet she is not come" and accuses the Nurse of being "<u>unwieldy, slow, heavy</u>".

2) Her use of imagery — such as "<u>wind-swift</u> Cupid wings" — also shows that she's <u>impatient</u> and can't wait to be married to Romeo.

3) There's a <u>comic contrast</u> between Juliet's wish for <u>speed</u> and the Nurse's <u>slowness</u> when she arrives.

4) Juliet becomes <u>frantic</u> for news. But the Nurse ignores the question and begins to complain about "how my head <u>aches</u>".

5) Their conversation is <u>funny</u>, but it's also shows their <u>loving relationship</u>. The Nurse obviously feels <u>close enough</u> to Juliet to <u>tease</u> her and it makes the scene quite <u>light-hearted</u>.

Scene Six — get your **Confetti** out

1) Scene Six is just before the wedding, and it's <u>very short</u>, which shows the audience how <u>rushed</u> the marriage is. There are no <u>wedding preparations</u> — they set off for the church as soon as Juliet arrives.

2) Shakespeare makes this scene feel <u>rushed</u>:

> The Friar begins to <u>rush</u> — he says "Come, come with me and <u>we will make short work</u>". This sounds as if he wants to get them married <u>as soon as possible</u>.

3) The Friar warns Romeo not to be in such a <u>rush</u> — "Too swift arrives as tardy as too slow". He tells Romeo to "<u>love moderately</u>" otherwise it won't be a "<u>long love</u>".

4) The Friar is also concerned that Romeo is showing <u>too much emotion</u> and that this is a <u>dangerous</u> sign — "These <u>violent delights</u> have <u>violent ends</u>".

© Moviestore Collection Ltd

Writer's Technique — Dramatic Irony

Romeo says let "<u>love-devouring death</u> do what he dare". This is <u>dramatic irony</u> because the <u>audience knows</u>, from the <u>prologue</u>, that <u>Romeo</u> and <u>Juliet</u> will <u>die</u>. Romeo's remark about death <u>builds</u> the <u>tension</u> — it's as if he's <u>tempting fate</u>.

Holy smoke — the deep fat Friar's gone up in flames...

Act 2 is the happiest bit of the play. Romeo and Juliet get married, and you almost forget it's all going to end in tears. But there are hints of trouble to come — like Tybalt challenging Romeo to a duel. There's no escaping that nasty feud.

Analysis of Act Three — Romeo is Banished

Well, I said there'd be fighting and here it is. Act Three is a real mixture of happy and sad bits.

Scene One — Two Deadly Swordfights

Key Scene

1) The scene starts off with a bit of <u>mood setting</u>. Benvolio says that the Capulets are "<u>abroad</u>" and uses <u>violent</u> images, such as "<u>mad blood stirring</u>". This increases the <u>tension</u>.

2) <u>Tybalt</u> appears. He wants to fight <u>Romeo</u> but Mercutio starts <u>teasing</u> him. The audience <u>doesn't know</u> who will end up in a duel, but they know that Tybalt's <u>aggressive</u> and good at <u>starting fights</u>.

3) Romeo tries to <u>stop</u> the fight by stepping between them — this shows how <u>desperate</u> he is to stop the conflict.

4) Romeo is struggling with his <u>divided loyalties</u>. He's trying to protect Tybalt <u>and</u> Mercutio (his best friend) — he's literally <u>caught in the middle</u> of the feud.

> **Writer's Technique — Dramatic Irony**
> The audience knows why Romeo <u>doesn't</u> want to fight (he's married to Tybalt's cousin, Juliet), but none of the <u>characters</u> do. Mercutio thinks Romeo's a <u>coward</u>, so he fights Tybalt <u>instead</u>.

> **Theme — Conflict**
> The <u>hatred</u> is so strong that Romeo can't stop the fighting.

Mercutio Dies

© John Haynes

Mercutio's death is <u>dramatic</u> because:

- It's a <u>shock</u>. Mercutio says it's only "a <u>scratch</u>".
- He's a <u>lively</u>, <u>funny</u> character — it's <u>sad</u> he dies.
- He wishes "a <u>plague</u> a' <u>both your houses!</u>" — he blames the <u>feud</u> for his death, and is <u>so angry</u> that he wants both families to <u>suffer</u> as he has.

Romeo wants to get Revenge

1) Romeo says "This but <u>begins</u> the <u>woe</u>" — fighting Tybalt will cause a lot of <u>trouble</u>, but he's <u>so angry</u> about Mercutio's death that he <u>doesn't care</u>.

2) He <u>refuses</u> to calm down — he wants to be "<u>fire-ey'd</u>", not forgiving. He <u>fights</u> and <u>kills Tybalt</u>.

> **Theme — Conflict**
> Romeo is usually <u>peaceful</u>, but when he's <u>angry</u> he's prepared to <u>kill</u>. The conflict makes even Romeo violent.

> **Turning Point in the action**
> Tybalt dies and Romeo is banished — he has to leave the city.

3) The Prince <u>banishes Romeo</u> from Verona. This causes a lot of <u>suspense</u> — it could <u>ruin everything</u> for Romeo and Juliet, but at least Romeo <u>hasn't</u> been punished with <u>death</u>.

Yesterday, love was such an easy game to play...

Hmm... everything gets messed up pretty quickly for young Romeo. One moment he's full of the joys of marrying Juliet, the next — his best mate is dead, his wife's cousin is dead and he's been kicked out of Verona. Sad times.

Analysis of Act Three — Everyone's Very Emotional

Juliet's **Torn** between **Love** and **Grief** in **Scene Two**

1) At the start of this scene, the <u>audience</u> knows that <u>Tybalt's dead</u> and <u>Romeo's banished</u>. But Juliet <u>hasn't</u> heard the news yet — she wants it to be "night <u>immediately</u>" so she can spend her wedding night with her husband.

2) The scene becomes very <u>dramatic</u> and full of <u>emotion</u>. E.g. the Nurse uses <u>dramatic images</u> such as "a <u>bloody piteous corse</u>" (corpse) and "all bedaub'd in <u>blood</u>".

3) Juliet's emotions are all over the place — she's <u>suicidal</u> when she thinks Romeo is dead, but <u>confused</u> when the Nurse mentions Tybalt, and then <u>angry</u> that "Romeo's hand shed Tybalt's blood".

4) Juliet's <u>confusion</u> is shown through the <u>images</u> she uses. She describes Romeo as a "<u>beautiful tyrant</u>, <u>fiend angelical</u>". She thinks he's <u>evil</u> but still <u>loves</u> him.

Theme — Family

This scene shows that Juliet cares for <u>Romeo</u> more than her <u>family</u> or her own <u>life</u>. She <u>forgives</u> Romeo for killing Tybalt, but when she remembers that Romeo's <u>banished</u> she becomes <u>suicidal</u>.

5) Juliet tries to be <u>strong</u> and <u>control</u> her emotions — "wherefore weep I then?". She realises that Tybalt "would have <u>slain</u>" <u>Romeo</u> if Romeo hadn't killed him, so she decides to stand by her husband.

Scene Three — Romeo would rather **Die** than **Leave** Juliet

1) Romeo thinks banishment has "<u>more terror</u>" than death, so this scene's a <u>rollercoaster</u> of <u>different emotions</u> as he struggles to cope with his punishment.

2) He uses <u>repetitive language</u> — he says "<u>banished</u>" or "<u>banishment</u>" many times in the scene, which shows that he's not thinking straight and is <u>completely overwhelmed</u>.

3) There are a lot of <u>similarities</u> between <u>Romeo</u> in this scene and <u>Juliet</u> in Act Three, Scene Two — Romeo becomes <u>suicidal</u> at the thought of living without "dear Juliet's hand".

© Moviestore Collection Ltd

4) The Friar convinces Romeo not kill himself and tells him to grow up — "Art thou a <u>man</u>?".

5) This reminds you that Romeo is still <u>young</u> — he <u>needs</u> the Friar to tell him what to do.

6) When Romeo leaves he's <u>happy</u> and <u>excited</u> about seeing Juliet — "a joy past joy". That's a pretty <u>sharp change</u> from suicidal — it suggests Romeo has <u>wild mood swings</u>.

... now Romeo needs a place to hide away...

What a rollercoaster of emotions — Juliet's upset cos Romeo has killed Tybalt. Romeo's upset cos he thinks he's ruined everything. Look at the imagery and language Shakespeare uses to show their emotions — it's pretty dramatic stuff.

Analysis of Act Three — Things get Worse for Juliet

This is getting complicated — skim back through to check the bits you're not clear about before you read on.

Scene Four — The Capulets and Paris set a Date

1) Capulet tells Paris that Juliet will marry him on <u>Thursday</u>, as he thinks she'll be "rul'd / In all respects" by him.

2) This is more <u>dramatic irony</u>. Juliet is <u>madly in love</u> with her <u>husband</u>, so the audience expects that Juliet will react <u>badly</u> to the news that she has to <u>marry someone else</u>.

3) The audience knows Juliet can't marry Paris when she's already married — it would be very <u>sinful</u>.

Turning Point in the action
Juliet has to get married to Paris in three days time — her family don't know she's already married to Romeo

4) But the <u>audience</u> has also just been told that <u>Capulet expects</u> her to react <u>obediently</u>. This <u>contrast</u> creates an atmosphere of <u>suspense</u>.

Scene Five starts with Romance...

1) Early next day Romeo <u>leaves</u> for <u>Mantua</u>. They <u>drag out</u> saying goodbye, but eventually Romeo has to go.

2) Shakespeare gives this scene a <u>bittersweet mood</u> — Juliet pretends it's not morning yet — "It was the <u>nightingale</u> and not the <u>lark</u>". She <u>desperately</u> wants him to stay.

3) The <u>romance</u> at the <u>start</u> of the scene makes Capulet's <u>rage</u> later on even more <u>shocking</u>.

4) There's also <u>foreshadowing</u> when Juliet says that Romeo looks like he's "<u>dead in the bottom of a tomb</u>".

Theme — Love

Romeo and Juliet appear <u>close</u> and <u>loving</u> — they understand each other's imagery and they speak in <u>rhyme</u> together — Juliet says "more <u>light</u> and <u>light</u> it grows", and Romeo finishes — "more <u>dark</u> and <u>dark</u> our woes".

... but soon Turns Nasty

1) Lady Capulet tells Juliet that's she's going to marry Paris, but she <u>refuses</u>, making her father <u>angry</u>.

2) Capulet <u>rants uncontrollably</u> — he speaks in short, sharp bursts — "hang! Beg! Starve! <u>Die</u> in the <u>streets</u>!" and insults Juliet — "green-sickness carrion... baggage... tallow-face".

3) Even the Nurse says that she should marry Paris. Juliet feels betrayed and calls her a "<u>wicked fiend</u>".

4) There are a lot of difficult <u>emotional</u> things for Juliet to cope with in this scene. By the end, the audience has seen <u>Romeo</u>, her <u>father</u>, her <u>mother</u> and the <u>Nurse</u> leave Juliet, until finally she is <u>alone</u> on the stage.

5) This is a strong <u>visual clue</u> that Juliet's <u>desperate</u>, and the Friar is her <u>last hope</u>.

© Moviestore Collection Ltd

Theme — Family

In those days, fathers expected <u>total obedience</u> from their daughters. Capulet's violence shows how <u>shocked</u> he is that she's challenging his <u>authority</u>.

Bigamy or suicide — not the best choice in the world...

Romeo's best friend's dead. Romeo and Juliet are married but can't be together for more than a night. Juliet's being made to marry a stranger. Not a very cheerful act really. Learn all the main events — it's sad stuff, but it's important.

Analysis of Act Four — Juliet is Desperate

Act Four's not even slightly happy, but the story's not hard to follow — Juliet's parents are frantic to get her married to Paris, and Juliet does everything she can to get out of it.

Scene One — Friar Lawrence's **Cunning Plan**

1) Juliet arrives at the Friar's just as Paris is leaving. This scene is very <u>tense</u> — the audience has just seen Juliet feeling <u>angry</u> and <u>suicidal</u>, but now she has to be <u>polite</u> to Paris.

2) As soon as Paris leaves, Juliet shows her <u>real feelings</u>. Her cry that she is "past hope, past cure, past help!" contrasts with her <u>controlled behaviour</u> with Paris. This makes her emotions more dramatic in <u>comparison</u>.

© Moviestore Collection Ltd

3) Juliet tells the Friar she would rather <u>kill herself</u> than marry Paris.

4) The Friar <u>has</u> to help — he's a <u>religious</u> man so he can't allow her to commit a <u>sin</u> by marrying a second time. He's also <u>responsible</u> for her secret marriage. He gives her a sleeping <u>potion</u> that will make her <u>look dead</u>.

> **Turning Point in the action**
> The Friar has come up with a plan — Juliet will fake her own death, and he'll write to Romeo. Then after she's buried, Romeo will rescue her.

Juliet plays the **Dutiful Daughter** in **Scene Two**

1) The Capulet household is <u>preparing</u> for the <u>wedding</u> — even though Juliet hasn't yet <u>agreed</u> to marry Paris. This shows the audience that Juliet's parents have <u>ignored</u> her pleas to not marry him.

2) Juliet tells her parents she's sorry she was <u>disobedient</u> and that she'll <u>marry Paris</u>.

3) Juliet's <u>behaviour</u> makes her character seem very <u>determined</u> — she <u>fools</u> her parents into thinking that she will be "<u>rul'd</u>" by them, so that she can get what she wants.

Scene Three has a **Dark** and **Desperate Mood**

1) Juliet gets ready to take the Friar's potion. She sends her mother and the Nurse away, but then she wants to "call them back to <u>comfort</u>" her — she feels <u>alone</u> and <u>scared</u>.

It's ironic that Juliet worries that she will wake up in the tomb before Romeo arrives. Actually the opposite happens — she wakes up too late.

2) Shakespeare develops an <u>atmosphere of fear</u> in Juliet's <u>speech</u>. She uses <u>horrible images</u> to describe the <u>tomb</u> — it has a "<u>foul mouth</u>" and Tybalt's body is "<u>festering</u>" there. She's worried she'll "<u>madly play</u>" with her ancestors bones.

> **Writer's Technique — Soliloquy**
> In a way this speech is Juliet's <u>farewell soliloquy</u>. She thinks about <u>death</u> and her <u>love for Romeo</u>, and it's her <u>last</u> big speech in the play.

I've got a bad feeling about this...

The Friar is helping Juliet out of a sticky situation here — but it's a risky plan. It's pretty brave of Juliet to take a potion that might kill her. I guess some people will do anything for love.

Analysis of Act Four — Juliet's Fake Death

Everything's still going according to the Friar's plan. If you're going to write about this scene in an essay, you need to know the plan and who's in on it and who's not.

Scene Four — A Happy, Busy Atmosphere

1) Capulet, Lady Capulet and the Nurse are preparing the house for the <u>wedding</u>.

2) The <u>atmosphere</u> is <u>rushed</u> but <u>jolly</u> — they're in a <u>good mood</u> about the party and happily <u>teasing</u> each other with names like "<u>cot-quean</u>" and "<u>jealous-hood</u>".

3) This jolliness <u>contrasts</u> sharply with the <u>dark atmosphere</u> of the previous scene. It also creates <u>suspense</u>, as the audience know that the Capulets are in for a <u>nasty shock</u>.

©20thC.Fox/Everett/Rex Features

Writer's Technique — Structure

This scene <u>mirrors</u> Act one scene five, when the Capulets were preparing for the ball. The <u>similarities</u> of the scenes remind the audience of their <u>different</u> positions in the play's <u>structure</u> — <u>then</u> the play was moving towards <u>romance</u>, but <u>now</u> it's accelerating into <u>tragedy</u> (see page 45 for more on structure).

In Scene Five the Capulets are Shocked and Upset

1) There's a <u>strange atmosphere</u> in this scene — the <u>audience</u> isn't supposed to feel <u>sad</u> because they know that Juliet isn't <u>really dead</u>, but everyone on <u>stage</u> is very <u>sad</u> and <u>emotional</u>

Theme — Family

The Capulets' <u>grief</u> suggests that they <u>loved</u> Juliet. But the audience knows that Juliet had to fake her own death to avoid being <u>forced</u> into marriage by her <u>family</u>.

2) The Nurse thinks Juliet is sleeping late — so there is <u>dramatic tension</u> as the audience waits for her to realise that Juliet is <u>apparently dead</u>.

3) Then Lady Capulet, Capulet and Paris are told that Juliet's dead, and they're all <u>very upset</u>.

Writer's Technique — Foreshadowing

Capulet describes Juliet's death using the image that "<u>Death</u>" is his "<u>son-in-law</u>". This <u>foreshadows</u> Juliet's true fate — her <u>marriage</u> will eventually lead to her <u>death</u>.

4) The ending is <u>quite strange</u> — Peter tries to get the musicians to play something cheerful. This bit's not <u>really</u> funny, but it could be there to give the audience a <u>rest</u> after all the <u>emotion</u>.

Theme — Love

This scene strongly <u>emphasises</u> a <u>link</u> between <u>love</u> and <u>death</u> — <u>death</u> becomes Juliet's <u>groom</u> and everything changes from "<u>wedding</u> cheer to a sad <u>burial</u> feast".

Poison — that's what Julie-ate...

I promise you this is dead important — learn who knows what as well as who does what. Like the Friar knows Juliet's not really dead but her parents and the Nurse having no idea — it explains why people do what they do.

Analysis of Act Five — The Plan Starts to Go Wrong

The last act! You're a mole's whisker away from the end. But don't start rushing just because it's the last act.

Scene One — Romeo Gets the **Wrong** end of the stick

1) Romeo is in Mantua. He <u>dreamt</u> that he was <u>dead</u>, and that Juliet brought him <u>back to life</u> with a <u>kiss</u>.

2) This <u>foreshadows</u> what happens at the end of the play, but Juliet's kisses <u>can't revive</u> Romeo.

3) Romeo's servant Balthasar tells Romeo that <u>Juliet is dead</u>. Romeo still <u>doesn't know</u> about the Friar's <u>plan</u>, so he thinks Juliet <u>really</u> is dead.

© AF archive / Alamy

Theme — Fate

This scene explores the importance of fate in Romeo's tragic death. It is purely fate that the letter didn't arrive, but Romeo's <u>impatience</u> is also part of his downfall. His decision to commit suicide might seem <u>rushed</u> and <u>foolish</u> — it doesn't even occur to him to contact the Friar.

4) Shakespeare includes two points to raise the audience's hopes — so they're kept in <u>suspense</u>. Balthasar tells him to "<u>have patience</u>", but Romeo <u>ignores</u> him. Romeo does ask if there are any <u>letters</u> to him "<u>from the Friar</u>", but there <u>aren't any</u>.

5) Romeo calls on an <u>apothecary</u> and bribes him to get poison so that he can kill himself in Juliet's tomb. This shows how <u>determined</u> he is to die — he takes advantage of the man's "<u>poverty</u>" to get what he wants.

Scene Two — the Friar's letter **Didn't** get through

Turning Point in the action
The Friar's letter wasn't delivered.

1) This scene <u>increases the tension</u> even more. The letter <u>wasn't delivered</u> — so there's <u>no chance</u> of Romeo finding out about the <u>plan</u>.

2) Friar Lawrence decides to <u>write to Romeo</u> again, and then go to the <u>tomb</u>. But Romeo is rushing to Verona to <u>kill himself</u>.

3) The Friar, who was supposed to be <u>in control</u> of the <u>risky plan</u>, has now <u>lost control</u> of the situation.

4) Shakespeare keeps the audience <u>hoping</u> — the Friar <u>might</u> meet Romeo at the tomb or Juliet <u>might</u> wake up <u>in time</u>. It seems <u>almost possible</u> that it'll all work out, even though you <u>know</u> from the <u>prologue</u> that it won't.

Writer's Technique — Dramatic Irony

Shakespeare uses a lot of <u>dramatic irony</u> here — each character is <u>ignorant</u> of one piece of <u>vital information</u>, and this <u>ignorance</u> is driving the plot closer to <u>tragedy</u>. However, the <u>audience</u> knows <u>everything</u> and can only sit there and watch as the characters head towards their <u>doom</u>.

If only he'd used recorded delivery...

In your essay, show you know the end of the play as well as you know the beginning. Some folks think they can get away with only knowing the beginning in detail. They're wrong. It doesn't matter which question you're answering — you have to know the whole plot or you'll say something daft.

Analysis of Act Five — Romeo Wants to Die

This is it, the last scene of the last act. There are only three scenes in Act 5, but to make up for it Scene 3's a whopper. It's full of misunderstandings and deaths — a proper tragedy.

Scene Three — Paris dies

Key Scene

1) Paris lays flowers at Juliet's tomb. When Romeo and his servant arrive, Paris hides.

2) Romeo tells his servant to leave, and threatens to tear him "joint by joint" if he stays. Shakespeare's language shows how determined Romeo is to die — he will kill anyone who gets in his way.

3) There's more dramatic irony here. Paris thinks that Romeo's going to vandalise the tomb, so he tries to arrest him.

4) This shows that Paris has feelings for Juliet — he wants to defend her honour. However, the audience knows that Paris's actions are pointless.

> **Theme — Love**
>
> This scene contrasts Romeo and Paris's love for Juliet. Paris is controlled and traditional — he calls Juliet a "sweet flower". Romeo is wild and angry. He calls the tomb a "detestable maw" that has eaten the "dearest morsel of the earth" — Juliet.

5) The audience also knows that Romeo's unstable and violent. It's very tense, because Romeo doesn't want to fight — he begs Paris to "tempt not a desperate man", but Paris won't leave so they fight and Romeo kills him.

6) As Paris dies he asks Romeo to lay him "with Juliet" — this suggests that he also loved Juliet.

... and then Romeo dies

1) In the tomb, Romeo's amazed that Juliet still looks so beautiful — "Death's pale flag is not advanced there".

> **Writer's Technique — Dramatic Irony**
>
> The audience knows how close Romeo is to realising that she isn't dead, but he doesn't know how true his own words are. This dramatic irony increases the sadness of the scene.

©SNAP/Rex Features

2) Romeo thinks fate is trying to keep him and Juliet apart, but death will bring them together. By dying he will "shake the yoke of inauspicious stars" and escape his fate.

> **Theme — Fate**
>
> Shakespeare doesn't say if it's fate or Romeo's character that leads him to death. It's left open to interpretation.

3) But the audience knows how wrong Romeo is — he was fated to die in Act 1 so actually he is doing exactly what he was doomed to do.

4) As he dies, he says "Here's to my love!" — this mirrors when Juliet drinks her potion — "Romeo!... I drink to thee".

Romeo's long speech is a soliloquy — he describes his emotions and thoughts so the audience knows exactly how he's feeling.

We'll always have Paris — oh wait, no we won't...

You gotta feel sorry for Paris. He doesn't do anything wrong in the play and he seems like a decent guy. At the end, he thinks Romeo is up to no good at the Capulet tomb and he dies defending Juliet's honour — because he loves her.

Analysis of Act Five — A Sad but Hopeful Ending

This scene is huge, and very complicated too. Take it in bite-sized chunks and it'll be easier to swallow.

... and *Juliet Dies* too

1) Friar Lawrence finds Paris and Romeo's bodies. His speech is full of <u>horrible images</u> of "<u>grubs</u> and <u>eyeless skulls</u>". This sets the <u>mood</u> of the scene — full of <u>death</u> and <u>horror</u>.

2) Juliet wakes up, and the Friar sounds <u>frightened</u> as he asks her to "Come, come away", then <u>runs away</u>. This cowardly behaviour <u>contrasts</u> with his previous wisdom and advice.

© Pictorial Press Ltd / Alamy

3) Juliet kisses Romeo's lips, hoping that "some <u>poison</u> yet doth hang on them" — this action reminds the audience that <u>death</u> and <u>love</u> are <u>linked</u> throughout the play.

4) Juliet gave a <u>speech</u> about <u>death</u> before she took the Friar's potion in Act 4 — so Shakespeare doesn't repeat it here. But because she doesn't have a long <u>soliloquy</u> before her suicide it also makes it seem <u>rushed</u> and <u>panicked</u> — she doesn't seem to <u>think</u> about what she's doing.

Finally, *Everyone* learns the *Truth*

1) The <u>Watch</u> (town guards), the <u>Prince</u>, Capulet and Lady <u>Capulet</u> arrive. The Watch explain that Paris and Romeo are dead, and Juliet is dead (again). <u>Montague</u> arrives and sees Romeo's body.

2) Most of the characters are on stage at this point — this creates a sense of <u>confusion</u> and <u>chaos</u>.

3) Also, everyone learns about the deaths at <u>different times</u>, and this <u>repetition</u> of Romeo and Juliet's fate highlights how many people have been affected.

4) Friar Lawrence explains the story, and says he should be <u>executed</u> if it's his <u>fault</u>. But he makes everything sound like a <u>big accident</u> so he can't be blamed.

5) You might think that a lot of what's happened is his fault, but the characters in the play don't seem to blame him.

> **Theme — Fate**
>
> Although the Prince <u>blames the feud</u>, he also says "<u>heaven</u> finds means to <u>kill your joys</u> with love" — which suggests that he also thinks <u>heaven</u> (another word for Fate) played an <u>important role</u> in the tragedy.

6) The Prince blames the feud for the deaths of <u>Romeo</u>, <u>Juliet</u>, <u>Mercutio</u> and <u>Paris</u> — but doesn't punish anyone. This suggests that the deaths of Romeo and Juliet are <u>punishment enough</u>.

7) Capulet and Montague <u>make peace</u>, and agree to put up a "<u>statue</u> in <u>pure gold</u>" in memory of Romeo and Juliet. So although it is a <u>tragedy</u>, the play has a <u>hopeful ending</u> as the violence is finally <u>over</u>.

Sniff, sigh — this story makes me tomb miserable...

That's it then, the complete story of *Romeo and Juliet*. Well now that you know what happens and what it all means you can swing on over to the next section and learn a bit more about the characters. My, my, the fun never stops...

Practice Questions

Blimey — I never knew 'Romeo and Juliet' was so long and fiddly-complicated. So, to make sure you know what actually happens in the play, try these revision questions — they're delicious. See if you can work through all of them without looking back over the section.

Quick Questions

1) Who stops the fighting in Act 1, Scene 1?

2) Why shouldn't Romeo and Benvolio be sneaking into Capulet's ball?

3) Why doesn't Tybalt fight Romeo at the ball?

4) In what scene do Romeo and Juliet meet for the first time?

5) What's the Friar's main reason for agreeing to marry Romeo and Juliet?

6) Who gets killed in Act 3, Scene 1? Who kills them?

7) Explain Friar Lawrence's plan to save Juliet from having to marry Paris.

8) Who does Romeo kill before he goes into the tomb, and why?

9) Who says they will put up a gold statue at the end of the play?

In-depth Questions

1) Do you think Paris and Rosaline are important characters? Explain why / why not.

2) Use examples from the play to describe the atmosphere during the balcony scene.

3) Look at Act 3, Scene 5. How does Shakespeare show Juliet's changing emotions to the audience?

4) Find a piece of dramatic irony in the play and explain how it might affect the audience.

5) Do you think Romeo is supposed to be an admirable character? Back up your ideas with quotes.

6) Think about the events below. Which event do you think is the turning point, where it all starts to go wrong? Explain your answer.

   a) Romeo and Juliet's wedding   b) Mercutio's death   c) Tybalt's death   d) The undelivered letter

Practice Questions

Exam-Style Questions

1 a) How does Shakespeare use language to make the passage below dramatic and tense?
   b) Explain how Shakespeare uses language in a different part of the play to create a dramatic mood.

Romeo:	This day's black fate on mo days doth depend:
	This but begins the woe others must end.
	Enter Tybalt
Benv.:	Here comes the furious Tybalt back again.
Romeo:	Again, in triumph, and Mercutio slain.
	Away to heaven respective lenity,
	And fire-ey'd fury be my conduct now!
	Now, Tybalt, take the 'villain' back again
	That late thou gav'st me, for Mercutio's soul
	Is but a little way above our heads,
	Staying for thine to keep him company.
	Either thou, or I, or both must go with him.
Tybalt:	Thou wretched boy, that didst consort him here,
	Shalt with him hence.
Romeo:	This shall determine that.
	They fight. Tybalt falls.
Benv.:	Romeo, away, be gone,
	The citizens are up, and Tybalt slain!
	Stand not amaz'd. The Prince will doom thee death
	If thou art taken. Hence, be gone, away!
Romeo:	O, I am fortune's fool.
	(Act 3, Scene 1)

Controlled Assessment-Style Questions

1 Show how Shakespeare explores the theme of death through language and events in *Romeo and Juliet*.

2 Explore how Shakespeare dramatises the theme of conflict in *Romeo and Juliet*.

With some exam boards, you might have to <u>compare</u> the play with <u>another</u> text in your controlled assessment. These practice questions are still useful — just remember to discuss <u>two texts</u> in your answer.

Character Profile — Romeo

A rose by any other name would smell as sweet — but you need to do a bit more than remember Romeo's name. If you learn a few points about what he's like, you can mention them in essays for juicy marks.

Romeo's **Romantic** and **Passionate**

1)   Romeo is a romantic character — he talks a lot about love.

2)   Romeo rushes into whatever his feelings tell him to do, which makes him seem passionate and easily swept up in emotions.

3)   When he falls in love with Juliet it happens instantly — and within 24 hours he's married to her.

Romeo is...

romantic: "Love is a smoke made with the fume of sighs"
hot-headed: "fire-ey'd fury be my conduct now!"
respected: "a virtuous and well-governed youth"

At first, Romeo is **In Love** with **Rosaline**

1)   At the start of the play, Romeo is "in sadness" because he thinks he's in love with Rosaline.

2)   Romeo's love for Rosaline seems childish and unrealistic. Friar Lawrence says "thy love did read by rote" — Romeo thinks he knows what love is from poems and books, but has never really experienced it.

3)   Mercutio mocks Romeo's habit of writing clichéd love poetry — "pronounce but 'love' and 'dove'" — which suggests Romeo's feelings for Rosaline weren't very real.

4)   Juliet says "you kiss by th'book" — perhaps he's a good kisser, but doesn't put much real feeling into it.

5)   At first, Romeo describes his feelings using images that seem clever but not very emotional — "O that I were a glove". Shakespeare does this to show that, early on in the play, Romeo knows more about the poetic language of love than the actual emotion.

Theme — Love

When Romeo thinks he's in love with Rosaline, his language is negative and glum. His love for Juliet makes him happy and excited — he uses images of brightness.

Romeo Develops during the Course of the Play

1)   Romeo becomes more realistic when he meets Juliet. He gives a "faithful vow" to have organised their wedding "by the hour of nine" — their relationship is more practical and real.

2)   His descriptions of feelings seem more honest — "the measure of thy joy be heap'd like mine".

3)   There are two ways of interpreting Romeo's relationship with Rosaline. Some people think that his immature attitude towards Rosaline makes his love for Juliet seem more powerful in comparison.

4)   Or you could say it proves that Romeo never properly loved — he's just a "young waverer" who falls in and out of love too easily.

Character Profile — Romeo

Romeo, Romeo, lots more stuff to learn about Romeo...

He can be *Funny* and *Intelligent*

1) Romeo's not always mooning about love. With his <u>friends</u>, his humour is "<u>most sharp</u>" and he makes a <u>rude pun</u> about "<u>my pump</u>". When Romeo is joking around, Mercutio says "<u>now art thou Romeo</u>" — which suggests he's usually more <u>fun</u>.

2) Shakespeare uses Romeo's <u>dialogues</u> with <u>Mercutio</u> to show his <u>sense of humour</u>, but also his <u>flaws</u>. Mercutio <u>teases</u> Romeo for being <u>too soppy</u>.

3) This makes their <u>friendship</u> seem strong — Mercutio is <u>close enough</u> to Romeo to be <u>brutally honest</u> — and reminds the audience that Romeo is <u>obsessed with love</u>, which is possibly his <u>biggest flaw</u>.

He's got a *Dangerous Side* too

1) Romeo's prepared to <u>fight</u> to the <u>death</u> to revenge Mercutio's death, which shows he's <u>loyal</u> and also has a <u>violent</u> side.

2) There's a big <u>contrast</u> between Romeo's actions when he is with Juliet and when he is fighting. Romeo says himself that Juliet has "<u>soften'd</u>" him.

3) This shows that he has <u>different sides</u>. But he is always <u>strong and passionate</u> — in violent duels as well as in love.

© Photos 12 / Alamy

Theme — Conflict

Romeo never fights without a reason, in contrast to a character like Tybalt, who always seems aggressive. But when Romeo does fight (out of <u>revenge</u> for Mercutio, or <u>grief</u> for Juliet) his violence is <u>wild</u> and <u>unstoppable</u>.

He *Loses His Head* a lot — and does *Stupid Things*

1) Romeo never seems to <u>think things through</u>. He's usually giving fancy descriptions of his feelings, or <u>rushing</u> about getting into <u>duels</u> and arranging <u>secret marriages</u>.

2) Other characters tell him to go "<u>Wisely and slow</u>" or to stop "<u>drivelling love</u>" — but he <u>doesn't listen</u> to their advice, which makes him seem <u>headstrong</u>.

3) Romeo believes in the power of fate and thinks he is "<u>fortune's fool</u>" — <u>controlled</u> by some greater force.

4) He's not completely <u>blameless</u>. He's partly a victim of fate and partly a victim of his own <u>impulsive actions</u>. For example, he doesn't stop to think before <u>killing</u> Tybalt.

Theme — Fate

Romeo thinks he can feel "Some <u>consequence</u> yet hanging <u>in the stars</u>" and worries that fate is against him. This <u>darkens</u> the atmosphere of the play, but also suggests that he won't accept <u>responsibility</u> for his own <u>decisions</u>.

---

*Romantic, passionate and fearless — *sigh*...*

So Romeo's not just a slushy character. He's a fighter, too. These are a few of the main points to get you started. There are loads of things you could say about Romeo — but remember to back it up with quotes.

Character Profile — Juliet

Soft, what light through yonder window breaks? It's Juliet, and you need to know what she's really like.

*Juliet is **Beautiful** and **Intelligent***

1) The other characters use images of <u>light</u> and <u>flowers</u> to <u>describe</u> Juliet — Romeo says she "<u>is the sun</u>" and her father calls her "the <u>sweetest flower</u> of all the field".

2) This shows that she is <u>bright</u> and <u>full of energy</u>, as well as <u>beautiful</u>.

3) She is <u>intelligent</u> and <u>witty</u> — in her conversations with Romeo she <u>criticises</u> the <u>poetic way</u> he talks.

4) She says that it's better to be "more <u>rich</u> in <u>matter</u> than in <u>words</u>" — meaning that <u>realistic</u>, <u>genuine love</u> is better than <u>clichés</u>.

Juliet is...

beautiful: "The brightness of her cheek would shame those stars"

romantic: "My bounty is as boundless as the sea,
My love as deep: the more I give to thee
The more I have, for both are infinite."

independent: "My dismal scene I needs must act alone."

brave: "Go, get thee hence, for I will not away."

If you get confused about who's from which <u>family</u>, this is a great way to remember:

Juli-ET Capul-ET

*Juliet changes after she meets **Romeo***

1) At the start of the play, she is <u>young</u> and <u>innocent</u>. She hasn't thought about marriage — it's "an honour that I <u>dream not</u> of". She obeys her parents, and agrees she'll "<u>look to like</u>" Paris as she's asked.

2) But meeting Romeo <u>changes her attitude</u> — she starts to think about what she wants, not what her parents want for her. She quickly becomes more <u>independent</u>, and stands up to her parents.

*She's **Impulsive** and **Passionate***

1) Juliet's <u>surprisingly forward</u> with Romeo — she lets him <u>kiss</u> her at the ball, when she doesn't even know his <u>name</u>.

© Moviestore Collection Ltd

2) She makes a <u>sexual pun</u> about "any other <u>part</u> / Belonging to a <u>man</u>" when she's thinking about Romeo — she feels <u>passionately</u> about him even though she's only just met him.

3) She knows that she's expected to hide her real feelings about Romeo — she apologises for being "too <u>quickly</u> won".

4) She quickly decides that Romeo is her "<u>true-love passion</u>", and once she feels that way, she's too <u>passionate</u> to control herself.

5) She's very <u>keen</u> to get married. She suggests it first and she rushes off to Friar Lawrence's when Romeo arranges the wedding.

6) Shakespeare's audiences would think that Juliet wasn't behaving <u>properly</u> for a <u>young lady</u> at that time.

Character Profile — Juliet

She's **Young** but **Determined**

1) Juliet's really young — "not <u>fourteen</u>".

2) Shakespeare <u>deliberately</u> made her <u>so young</u> to make her impulsive, passionate behaviour more <u>shocking</u> to audiences at the time.

3) Juliet's youth makes her attitude seem <u>surprisingly wise</u> and <u>strong</u> — she wisely says that love should be "<u>ripening</u>" instead of "<u>too sudden</u>".

4) She also won't let herself cry "<u>foolish tears</u>" when Romeo is <u>banished</u>, which shows her character's <u>strength</u>.

©20thC.Fox/Everett/Rex Features

She has a **Lot** to **Cope With**

Theme — Love

You can make your own mind up about the <u>love</u> between Romeo and Juliet in this play. Some people think that the play portrays a love so <u>strong</u> that <u>nothing else matters</u>. Others think it's <u>immature madness</u>.

1) Juliet's character also seems <u>inexperienced</u>. At only thirteen, she has to deal with an <u>arranged marriage</u>, a <u>secret love</u>, the <u>death</u> of a cousin, a fake <u>suicide</u> and the death of her <u>husband</u>.

2) You could say that Juliet's decisions to get married in secret and to fake her own death are <u>immature</u> and she just gets <u>carried away</u> with love.

3) Or maybe she's <u>brave</u> and copes well with <u>difficult situations</u>. It depends on your <u>point of view</u>.

Juliet's **Actions Reveal** a lot about her **Character**

1) Whether her actions are <u>brave</u> or <u>foolish</u>, they definitely show that Juliet isn't a <u>weak</u>, <u>submissive</u> character.

2) She marries for love, <u>defying</u> her parents and risking being <u>outcast</u> by her entire family for loving their enemy.

3) She's <u>loyal</u> to Romeo even though he kills her cousin — which suggests she's a <u>forgiving</u> character.

Context — Women's place in society

It'd take a lot more <u>guts</u> to get married secretly in Shakespeare's time. Juliet's <u>rebelling</u> against society's expectations and her family. Her parents would've been <u>very angry</u>, which is why she doesn't tell them.

4) She seems <u>moral</u> because she does what she thinks is <u>right</u>, even if it gets her into trouble. For example, she <u>refuses</u> to marry Paris. She's already married, so it would be <u>illegal</u> and <u>morally wrong</u>.

5) She drinks the potion that Friar Lawrence gives her, even though she's <u>scared</u> of waking up in a tomb with "<u>loathsome smells</u>". It's the only way to get what she wants, so this makes her seem <u>determined</u> and brave.

Juliet's brave — she puts up with that Nurse...

So, Juliet's a feisty independent lady, but she's also an immature love-sick teenager. She breaks social conventions but has high moral standards. Phew. Sounds like perfect essay material to me. Although maybe not the perfect girlfriend...

Character Profile — Mercutio

I know it's a silly name, but he's related to the Prince — so I wouldn't mess with him if I were you...

Mercutio is Romeo's **Best Mate**

1) Mercutio is Romeo's <u>best friend</u>.

2) He goes with him to the ball, and tries to cheer him up with a <u>speech</u> about "<u>Queen Mab</u>" — a fairy who brings dreams.

3) The speech shows a lot about Mercutio — it's full of <u>puns</u> and <u>innuendos</u>, to show how <u>intelligent</u> and <u>witty</u> he is.

> **Mercutio is...**
>
> **lively:** "You have dancing shoes
> With nimble soles"
>
> **talkative:** "Peace, peace, Mercutio, peace.
> Thou talk'st of nothing."

4) He <u>criticises Romeo</u>, who believes <u>dreams</u> show the <u>future</u>. He says soldiers dream of "<u>cutting foreign throats</u>" and lovers "<u>dream of love</u>" — so dreams depend on the dreamer. This shows that Mercutio is a more <u>down-to-earth</u> character.

He's **Always Mocking** other **Characters**

1) Mercutio's bursting with <u>energy</u> and always making jokes or <u>teasing</u> someone.

2) For example, he calls Tybalt "<u>King of Cats</u>" and "<u>rat-catcher</u>" to wind him up. This name comes from a story with a <u>cat</u> character called <u>Tibalt</u>, that was popular at the time.

3) His speeches are full of <u>wordplay</u>, and <u>crazy ideas</u>, even when he knows he's dying — "Ask for me tomorrow, and you shall find me a grave man."

> **Theme — Love**
>
> Mercutio's attitude towards love is <u>cynical</u> and a <u>bit rude</u> — he tells Romeo to stop being so soppy. He also makes a lot of <u>sexual jokes</u>, which <u>contrast</u> with Romeo's <u>romantic</u> view of love.

Mercutio's playing on the double meaning of the word "grave" ("<u>serious</u>" and also a place where you put <u>dead people</u>).

Mercutio's the **First Person** to **Die** in the play

1) When Mercutio's killed it leaves a <u>big gap</u> in the <u>play</u>. All that <u>energy</u> suddenly <u>disappears</u>.

2) It's an important turning point — it "<u>begins</u> the <u>woe</u>" of tragic events in the rest of the play.

3) He wishes "a <u>plague</u> o' <u>both</u> your houses" as he dies — this reminds the audience how <u>dangerous</u> the feud is.

4) It also <u>warns</u> the audience that more suffering will happen. Mercutio's <u>curse</u> comes true — partly because of his death, which <u>provokes</u> Romeo to kill Tybalt in <u>revenge</u>.

> **Theme — Honour**
>
> Mercutio should have been able to walk away from the fight, but he died because he was fighting to <u>protect</u> Romeo's <u>honour</u>. Maybe Shakespeare was <u>criticising</u> the importance of honour and showing how <u>pointless</u> it is.

Mercutio — doesn't that come before Venus...

The really important thing about Mercutio is he fills up the stage whenever he's on it with his nutty ideas and jokes. He even brings out the jokey side of Romeo. The jokes aren't all side-splitters, but you can't say he doesn't try.

Character Profile — Tybalt & Benvolio

You've got to get these characters clear in your head — strange names and all.

Tybalt is a Troublemaker

1) Tybalt is Juliet's <u>cousin</u>, and Lady Capulet's <u>nephew</u>.

2) In Act 1 he <u>insists</u> on fighting Benvolio.

3) He wants to <u>fight Romeo</u> at the ball, but Capulet says Romeo "<u>shall be endur'd</u>".

4) He challenges Romeo to a <u>duel</u>, but when Romeo <u>refuses</u> he fights <u>Mercutio</u> instead.

5) He <u>kills Mercutio</u> but then Romeo kills him in revenge.

> **Tybalt is...**
>
> **aggressive:** "... talk of peace? I hate the word"
> **loyal:** "Now by the stock and honour of my kin"

He Really Hates the Montagues

1) Tybalt is always <u>starting fights</u> with the Montagues — you could say he cared a lot about his <u>family's honour</u>, or maybe he's just <u>mean</u>.

2) He's got a nicer side too. The nurse calls him an "<u>honest gentleman</u>" and "the <u>best friend</u> I had". Juliet, her mother and the Nurse are really <u>upset</u> about him dying.

3) But he's portrayed as <u>very aggressive</u> and a cheat — he stabs Mercutio <u>under</u> Romeo's arm. The audience know this isn't fair — Tybalt is fighting dirty.

©Tony Larkin/Rex Features

> **Theme — Honour**
>
> Shakespeare uses Tybalt's character to show how <u>destructive</u> honour can be if it's taken to <u>extremes</u>.

Benvolio's a Nice bloke — he Doesn't get killed

1) Benvolio is Romeo's <u>cousin</u>. In Act 1 he tries to avoid fighting Tybalt but gets drawn into a fight anyway.

2) He <u>tries</u> to cheer Romeo up by <u>persuading</u> him to go to the Capulets' ball.

3) Benvolio tells Romeo to "<u>be gone, away!</u>" after he's killed Tybalt, and stays to <u>explain</u> what's happened to the Prince. His actions show that he's a <u>good friend</u>.

4) Benvolio usually <u>avoids conflict</u> — he's a peaceful character who tries to do the <u>right thing</u> and stay <u>out of trouble</u>.

> **Benvolio is...**
>
> **peaceful:** "I do but keep the peace, put up thy sword"
> **kind:** "What sadness lengthens Romeo's hours?"

> **Theme — Conflict**
>
> The <u>contrast</u> between Benvolio and Tybalt shows that the anger of the feud is <u>impossible</u> to stop. Benvolio tries to be <u>peaceful</u>, but Tybalt's <u>aggression</u> is stronger.

Tybalt = bad, Benvolio = good...

Tybalt and Benvolio are very different. Benvolio is sweet and tries to be peaceful — Tybalt is a pain and loves starting fights. Hmm... It's almost as if Shakespeare wrote the characters to be the exact opposite of each other. Funny that...

Character Profile — The Montagues

These are Romeo's mum and dad. Make sure you don't get them muddled up with Juliet's.

Montague *is Romeo's* Father — Head *of the* Montague *family*

1) Montague can be violent and angry — when he sees Capulet he wants to <u>fight</u> him, but his wife holds him back.

2) The Montagues and the Capulets are <u>fighting each other</u>, and Montague doesn't seem to have done much to stop this.

© John Haynes

3) But he also <u>worries</u> about Romeo when he's unhappy and would "<u>willingly give cure</u>" to cheer him up, which shows he is a kind father.

4) At the end of the play Montague and Capulet agree to <u>give up</u> the feud. This could be seen as <u>peaceful</u>, or <u>stubborn</u>. It suggests that <u>only</u> the death of their children is <u>shocking enough</u> to force them to end their "<u>enmity</u>".

5) After Romeo and Juliet are dead, Montague plans to "raise her <u>statue</u> in <u>pure gold</u>" to honour Juliet.

> **Montague is...**
>
> **a concerned father:** "Could we but learn from whence his sorrows grow"
> **Capulet's enemy:** "Thou villain Capulet!"

Lady Montague *is* Peaceful

1) Lady Montague <u>stops</u> Montague from fighting at the beginning of the play.

> **Lady Montague is...**
>
> **peaceful:** "Thou shalt not stir one foot to seek a foe."
> **emotional:** "Grief of my son's exile hath stopp'd her breath."

2) She's <u>worried</u> about Romeo and <u>relieved</u> that he "<u>was not at this fray</u>".

3) When Romeo's banished to Mantua it makes Lady Montague so unhappy that she <u>dies of grief</u>.

But the Montagues *are still* Involved *in the* Violent Feud

1) You don't see much of the <u>Montagues</u> — the Capulets are much more significant characters.

2) But Romeo's parents do have two <u>important roles</u> within the play:

> • Montague's kind to his family, but he's <u>blinded</u> by his <u>hatred</u> of Capulet and doesn't see that the feud is <u>foolish</u> and <u>dangerous</u>. He's just as <u>responsible</u> for the <u>conflict</u> as Capulet.
>
> • The Montagues also provide a <u>contrast</u> to the Capulets — who are <u>bossy</u>, <u>overbearing</u> and <u>very involved</u> in Juliet's life. The Montagues seem kinder but also more <u>detached</u> and <u>distant</u>.

They seem nice — but they're just as bad...

It's easy to think of the Montagues as goodies and the Capulets as baddies but unfortunately it's not that simple. Montague joins in with the feud just as happily as the Capulets do. And they don't give young Romeo much guidance.

Character Profile — The Capulets

Time to find out about Juliet's mum and dad. The Capulets aren't such a lovely couple.

Lady Capulet is Bossy and Ambitious

1) Lady Capulet is <u>materialistic</u>. She wants Juliet to gain <u>wealth</u> and <u>status</u> by marrying Paris.

2) She got married <u>young</u>, so she thinks it's fine for Juliet to do the same.

> **Lady Capulet is...**
>
> **ambitious:** "share all that he doth possess"
>
> **unforgiving:** "We will have vengeance for it"

© John Haynes

3) She wants to have Romeo <u>killed</u> as <u>punishment</u> for killing Tybalt — she can be <u>violent</u> and <u>unforgiving</u>.

4) She isn't a great <u>mother</u>. She asks the Nurse to "<u>come back</u> again" when she's <u>talking</u> to Juliet — this suggests that she's not used to being <u>alone</u> with Juliet and <u>relies</u> on the Nurse to do most of the <u>parenting</u>.

5) She's not <u>sympathetic</u> when Juliet is <u>upset</u> — she says it "shows still some <u>want</u> of <u>wit</u>" to cry so much.

> **Theme — Love**
>
> Lady Capulet has a <u>cold attitude</u> towards love and marriage — she only talks about Paris's <u>social position</u> and <u>wealth</u>, and never thinks about Juliet's <u>feelings</u>.

6) She rejects Juliet when she disobeys her — she says "I have <u>done</u> with <u>thee</u>" when Juliet begs for help.

7) She only <u>forgives Juliet</u> because she agrees to marry Paris.

Capulet is Lovely to Juliet — but Only If she Obeys him

1) Capulet <u>changes</u> during the play. At first, he wants to give Juliet a "scope of <u>choice</u>" in who she marries, and thinks she's a bit young to marry yet.

2) But when Juliet says she doesn't want to marry Paris, he's furious. He calls her a "<u>disobedient wretch</u>". This shows he's a <u>controlling character</u> — he doesn't like it when things don't go his way.

> **Context — Women's place in society**
>
> Juliet's <u>relationship</u> with her parents shows a lot about the way <u>women</u> were <u>expected</u> to behave in the 16th century. They '<u>belonged</u>' to their father or husband, like land or money, and were expected to do as they were <u>told</u>.

> **Capulet is...**
>
> **bossy:** "Peace, you mumbling fool!"
>
> **violent:** "My fingers itch."

3) It's a <u>powerful scene</u> — Juliet is begging for understanding — the <u>stage directions</u> say "*She <u>kneels</u> down*". But even though she's pleading with them, her parents don't give in.

4) The Capulets <u>represent</u> the kind of parents that Shakespeare's audience would <u>recognise</u> — <u>controlling</u> and <u>unsympathetic</u>. This helps the audience <u>relate</u> more to Juliet's <u>unhappiness</u>.

Well, OK, maybe these two ARE worse...

It's a good idea to learn quotes and examples about the characters — so you can back up the points you make in your essay. It shows you're not just making things up and that you genuinely know the play. Examiners love that...

Character Profile — Nurse

Right, this is where it gets a bit weird. Juliet's got a Nurse — only really she's more like a nanny.

The **Nurse** is Juliet's **Nanny**

1) The Nurse has <u>looked after</u> Juliet since she was a baby, and even did the breast-feeding.

2) The Nurse helps Romeo and Juliet arrange their marriage by <u>delivering messages</u> between them.

3) At the beginning of the play, the Nurse and Juliet are very <u>close</u>, but by the end they have been <u>driven apart</u>.

> **The Nurse is...**
>
> **affectionate**: "Thou wast the prettiest babe that e'er I nurs'd"
>
> **vulgar**: "Now by my maidenhead at twelve year old"

© John Haynes

The Nurse **Talks Too Much** — but she really **Loves** Juliet

1) Once the Nurse starts talking it's really hard to <u>stop</u> her — she's a <u>comedy character</u>.

2) The Nurse is <u>affectionate</u> with Juliet. She has <u>pet names</u> for her, like "<u>lamb</u>", "<u>ladybird</u>", and "<u>pretty fool</u>".

3) Juliet is much <u>closer</u> to the Nurse than to her mother — she tells the Nurse her <u>secrets</u>.

4) When Juliet seems to be dead, the Nurse seems more <u>genuinely upset</u> than any of the other characters — "Never was seen so black a day as this."

She seems to be an **Irresponsible Role Model**

1) The Nurse is more of a <u>mother figure</u> to Juliet than Lady Capulet, but she isn't always <u>responsible</u>.

2) The Nurse wishes Juliet to have "<u>happy nights to happy days</u>" — she focuses on Juliet's <u>sexual happiness</u>.

3) She helps Juliet marry Romeo even though she knows it's risky. But Juliet's <u>father</u> is the <u>boss</u> — and Juliet's only 13.

4) She doesn't think about long term <u>emotions</u> or the <u>danger</u> of the marriage.

> **Theme — Love**
>
> The Nurse makes <u>sexual</u> jokes and puns, such as "you shall bear the <u>burden</u> soon at <u>night</u>" — this brings <u>humour</u> to the play. She represents a <u>physical</u> attitude towards love that <u>contrasts</u> with Juliet's <u>innocent romance</u>.

5) When Juliet's being forced to marry Paris, the Nurse says it's "<u>best</u> you <u>married</u> with the <u>County</u>" — she's changed her mind from earlier, when she was encouraging Juliet and Romeo.

6) It's <u>practical advice</u> — it'd be <u>safer</u> for Juliet to <u>forget</u> about Romeo. But it shows that the Nurse <u>doesn't understand</u> how <u>strongly</u> Juliet loves Romeo, and <u>doesn't care</u> that Juliet would be committing a <u>sin</u>.

Just get to the... er... you know... sharp thingy, what's it called...

The Nurse waffles on a bit, repeats herself, and waffles on a bit... but she does her best for Juliet. She's also a funny character — Okay, she's no sharp-witted comedian, but she'd have had Shakespeare's audiences rofling in the aisles.

Character Profile — Friar Lawrence

A friar is a sort of monk, who does some of the things priests do — he can perform weddings, and people go to see him with their problems. This Friar also hands out plants and potions with special powers. Hmm...

The **Friar** Gives **Advice** to Romeo and Juliet

1) Friar Lawrence is a <u>father figure</u> to Romeo — he knows about Rosaline, which suggests Romeo <u>confides</u> in him.

2) He gives Romeo a lot of advice, and <u>persuades</u> him not to kill himself.

3) Juliet calls him a "<u>holy man</u>" and asks for help "in thy <u>wisdom</u>". He comes up with the plan for her to <u>fake</u> her <u>death</u>.

4) He knows a lot about <u>herbs</u>, and gives Juliet a drug that makes her appear dead.

5) At the end, when Juliet refuses to go with him, he <u>runs away</u> and leaves her in the tomb by herself.

> **The Friar is...**
>
> **respected**: "O Lord, I could have stayed here all the night
> To hear good counsel."
>
> **wise**: "love moderately; long love doth so."

Friar Lawrence seems **Helpful** and **Sensible**

1) Friar Lawrence seems quite <u>sensible</u> —he's surprised that Romeo has "so soon <u>forsaken</u>" Rosaline and moved on to Juliet.

2) The Friar <u>thinks things through</u>. For example, at first he is <u>against</u> Romeo's marriage to Juliet, but then he realises that it "may so <u>happy</u> prove" that it ends the feud.

3) He's the <u>voice of common sense</u> in the play.

4) He's also the <u>only one</u>, apart from Romeo and Juliet, who knows <u>exactly</u> what's going on, but he can't <u>stop</u> it going <u>wrong</u>.

© Tony Larkin/Rex Features

But he does some **Suspicious Things**...

1) Although Shakespeare <u>initially</u> presents the Friar as <u>fatherly</u> and <u>wise</u>, some of his actions could be seen as <u>irresponsible</u>. He's <u>not</u> always a good role model.

2) The Friar's decision to help Romeo and Juliet is <u>questionable</u> — he uses their love to try to <u>force</u> the Montagues and Capulets to change their "<u>rancour</u> to <u>pure love</u>".

3) You could argue that this means he doesn't <u>do what's best</u> for Romeo and Juliet. He warns "These <u>violent delights</u> have <u>violent ends</u>", but marries them anyway.

4) His plans are <u>risky</u>. Faking Juliet's death is an <u>extreme</u> and <u>dangerous</u> idea.

> **The Friar is...**
>
> **reckless**: "I do spy a kind of hope
> which craves as desperate an execution"
>
> **cowardly**: "I dare no longer stay."

5) He's also <u>cowardly</u> — he <u>abandons</u> Juliet in the tomb because he doesn't want to get into trouble.

6) There's no <u>right</u> or <u>wrong</u> answer about the Friar — you can <u>make up your own mind</u>, as long as you can find <u>quotes</u> to <u>support</u> your opinion.

Oops you're both dead — told you so...

Beware men in robes who think they know best. The Friar loves it when a plan comes together — unfortunately his madcap plans don't save the day. If anything, they make the day a bit of a bloodbath. At least he tried, bless him.

Character Profile — Paris, Prince & Others

Here's the last lot of characters to get to know, so get stuck in.

Paris Wants to *Marry Juliet*

1) Paris is a <u>rich</u> and <u>influential</u> nobleman. He's related to the Prince who rules Verona.

2) He keeps his emotions <u>hidden</u>. For example, when he visits Juliet's tomb he doesn't let his feelings <u>flood out</u> the way Romeo does.

3) When Paris is dying, he asks Romeo to put him in the tomb <u>with</u> Juliet. That shows a <u>bit</u> more emotion and suggests that his love for Juliet is genuine.

Paris's title is 'County', which means the same thing as a Count — a high-ranking nobleman. Just call him Paris.

Paris is...

respectable: "The gallant, young, and noble gentleman"

polite: "But now my lord, what say you to my suit?"

Theme — Love

Paris is <u>Romeo's rival</u> for Juliet's love. He represents a different, more <u>conventional</u> type of love. He asks Juliet's father for permission and is polite. Romeo seems more <u>passionate</u> and <u>wild</u> by comparison. However, Paris ends up dying for his love of Juliet too — Romeo <u>stabs him</u> when they fight at her tomb.

The *Prince* is the *Police Chief*, *Judge* and *Jury*

1) The Prince <u>rules</u> Verona so he always turns up to <u>sort things out</u> when there's been trouble or fighting.

2) He decides <u>who</u> gets punished and <u>how</u> — he demands that they "<u>Throw</u> your mistemper'd weapons to the ground and hear the <u>sentence</u> of your <u>moved prince</u>".

Theme — Conflict

Even though he's very powerful, the Prince can't escape the <u>violence</u> of the feud and he can't stop it. His <u>relatives</u> Paris and Mercutio get <u>killed</u> — which highlights how strong the feud is.

3) His role in the play is to be the one figure with <u>authority</u> over the Montagues and Capulets, so he speaks in really <u>formal</u> poetry — it makes him sound <u>posher</u> and more <u>powerful</u>.

And Finally, a couple of *Servants*...

1) There are two other characters you should just learn the names of — <u>Balthasar</u> is Romeo's servant, and <u>Peter</u> is a servant of the Capulets who helps the Nurse.

2) There are lots of other characters in the play — musicians, servants, and townspeople. You can think of them like <u>extras</u> in a film — just <u>concentrate</u> on the stars.

© PARAMOUNT / THE KOBAL COLLECTION

Paris — nice and polite but normal, boring and, ultimately, dead...

You don't need to know as much about these guys as you do about Romeo and Juliet — but you do need to know who they are, what they do in the play and why they do it. And maybe a couple of quotes. It'll be worth it in the end.

Practice Questions

If you don't know who's who in the play it can get seriously confusing. You need to know the names of all the main characters — and how to spell them. What's more, you've got to know what they're like, the main events they get involved in, and why they do the things they do. Keep going through these questions, looking up ones you don't know, until you can answer them all without cheating. Answer them all, I said.

Quick Questions

1) Write down the full names of Romeo and Juliet.

2) What does Romeo do that shows he can be dangerous?

3) Describe three brave things Juliet does in the play.

4) Which three words best describe Mercutio?
   a) funny b) intelligent c) peaceful   d) energetic   e) romantic

5) Who are the deadly enemies of the Montagues?

6) Apart from Romeo, who is Juliet closest to?

In-depth Questions

1) Describe Mercutio's character, using quotes to back up your answer.

2) How does Shakespeare use the characters of Benvolio and Tybalt to show the feud between the two families?

3) Explain Friar Lawrence's role in the play. Do you think he has a positive or negative effect?

4) What's Romeo like before he meets Juliet, and how does he change when he's in love with her?

5) Do you think the Montagues are good parents? Explain why, using examples from the play.

6) Explain Juliet's relationship with her parents, and how it changes through the play.

7) How does Juliet respond when the Nurse tells her to marry Paris? Do you think her feelings are justified? Back up your ideas with quotes.

Practice Questions

Well, enough of that easy-peasy warm-up stuff. Now it's time to show off your sparkling skills of eloquence, insight and general fabulousness with these exam-style questions. Enjoy...

Exam-Style Questions

1   a)   How does Shakespeare present the relationship between the Nurse and Juliet in the passage below.

    b)   Explore how the relationship between the Nurse and Juliet is presented in a different part of the play.

> **Juliet**:   I'faith I am sorry that thou art not well.
>
>   Sweet, sweet, sweet Nurse, tell me, what says my love?
>
> **Nurse**:   Your love says like an honest gentleman,
>
>   And a courteous, and a kind, and a handsome,
>
>   And I warrant a virtuous — Where is your mother?
>
> **Juliet**:   Where is my mother? Why, she is within.
>
>   Where should she be? How oddly thou repliest.
>
>   'Your love says, like an honest gentleman,
>
>   "where is your mother?"'
>
> **Nurse**:   Oh God's lady dear,
>
>   Are you so hot? Marry, come up, I trow.
>
>   Is this the poultice for my aching bones?
>
>   Henceforward do your messages yourself.
>
> **Juliet**:   Here's such a coil. Come, what says Romeo?
>
> **Nurse**:   Have you got leave to go to shrift today?
>
> **Juliet**:   I have.
>
> **Nurse**:   Then hie you hence to Friar Lawrence' cell.
>
>   There stays a husband to make you a wife.
>
>   Now comes the wanton blood up in your cheeks.
>
>   They'll be in scarlet straight at any news.
>
>   (Act 2, Scene 5, 54-72)

Controlled Assessment-Style Questions

1   Explore how Mercutio is presented using the way he speaks and his relationships with others.

2   Show how Shakespeare presents Romeo by contrasting him with the character of Tybalt.

3   Explore how Shakespeare portrays the characters of Capulet and Tybalt, and their relationship.

> With some exam boards, you might have to <u>compare</u> the play with <u>another</u> text in your controlled assessment. These practice questions are still useful — just remember to discuss <u>two texts</u> in your answer.

Religion

Religion was a much bigger part of daily life when Shakespeare wrote *Romeo and Juliet*.
Lovely William made it a big part of the play too.

The **Church** Had a **Big Influence** in the 16th Century

1) In Shakespeare's time, <u>everybody</u> had to go to church on Sunday. Anyone who didn't go had to pay a fine.

2) <u>No one</u> could get married <u>except</u> in church. Couples couldn't <u>live together</u> unless they got married, and they weren't meant to <u>sleep together</u> either. Divorce was almost <u>impossible</u>.

3) In some ways, religion was <u>more powerful</u> than the <u>law</u>. Religion provided an accepted set of <u>rules</u> for people to live their lives by.

Have a look on p.53 for some examples of religious imagery.

Religion is a **Powerful Force** in the **Play**

1) Romeo and Juliet live in quite a <u>religious</u> society. They have to live by the <u>moral rules</u> set by the Church.

2) For example, <u>getting married</u> is the <u>only option</u>. There's no other way they can be together, and their love is <u>so strong</u> that they'll do anything to be together.

3) Once Juliet's married to Romeo, the audience knows that she <u>can't</u> marry Paris. If she did, she'd be breaking the <u>law</u> of the Church and would go to hell.

4) However, both Romeo and Juliet commit <u>suicide</u> — and suicide was a <u>sin</u>.

The **Friar** represents the **Role** of the **Church** in **Verona**

1) The characters' <u>respect</u> for the Church is shown through their relationship with <u>Friar Lawrence</u>. The only time the Capulets allow Juliet out alone is when she's going "to Lawrence' cell, / to make <u>confession</u>". This shows that they <u>trust</u> the Friar and think confession is very <u>important</u>.

2) Romeo and Juliet <u>respect his advice</u> more than anyone else's. They're <u>rebellious</u> enough to defy their <u>parents</u> — but they usually follow all of the Friar's plans, however risky.

3) The Friar's <u>religious vows</u> mean he <u>has</u> to help Romeo and Juliet in certain ways. He <u>isn't allowed</u> to tell anybody the things he hears in <u>confession</u>, so he has to keep everything <u>secret</u>. Marriage is <u>sacred</u> to the Church, so he has to <u>protect their marriage</u> and help Juliet <u>escape</u> marriage to Paris.

Romeo & Juliet — a marriage made in... well, Verona...

When you're writing essays remember to show off a bit — show you understand the religious reasons for Romeo and Juliet getting married, and why Friar Lawrence tries to help them out. Keep a couple of quotes handy just in case...

Family and Marriage

OK, things have changed since Shakespeare's time. You've got to remember that lots of these things weren't strange then, although they seem pretty bizarre now.

Sometimes **Marriage** was for **Money,** not **Love**

1) In the 16th century, rich people like the Capulets <u>didn't</u> get married for <u>love</u>. Their parents arranged a marriage with someone rich and powerful. It was a <u>business deal</u> — a way of getting money or power.

2) Normally the bride and groom <u>didn't</u> get a <u>choice</u>. They were <u>told</u> they <u>had</u> to get married, just like Juliet.

3) Juliet is Lord Capulet's <u>only heir</u>. Capulet's rich, so she would be quite a catch for Paris.

4) The Capulets' <u>family structure</u> is fairly <u>typical</u> of what was expected in Shakespeare's time. The husband is in control of his wife and daughter, so Capulet can tell Juliet to marry whoever he wants.

> **Context —Women's place in society**
>
> When Juliet <u>refuses</u>, Capulet is <u>furious</u> — he sees her as his <u>property</u>, so she should do as he says. He also thinks he's done his duty and set her up with a good match — so he may be hurt as well.

Juliet **Rebels** against the **Family Structure**

1) Juliet's position in the <u>family</u> restricts her. She's a <u>young</u>, <u>unmarried daughter</u> so she can't be in public <u>unaccompanied</u>, or leave without permission.

2) This conflicts with what she actually <u>wants</u> to do — Juliet struggles to make her <u>parents</u> happy and make <u>herself</u> happy.

3) She doesn't <u>want</u> to upset her parents — but the family structure <u>forces</u> her to rebel.

4) The audience would've <u>easily related</u> to this theme. Many people during Shakespeare's time experienced this <u>conflict</u> between family <u>duty</u> and personal <u>happiness</u>, so they'd have understood Juliet's difficulties.

© Moviestore Collection Ltd

Romeo and Juliet's **Love Conflicts** with the **Family Feud**

1) The <u>family feud</u> creates a lot of <u>tension</u> in the play. Romeo and Juliet can't be together — their families are <u>enemies</u> and they'd never be <u>allowed</u> to get married.

2) The <u>contrast</u> between the <u>violent conflict</u> and their <u>love</u> makes their love seem even more <u>passionate</u> — the <u>harder</u> it is for them to be together, the more they <u>fight</u> and <u>struggle</u> to get what they want.

> **Theme — Conflict**
>
> <u>Family</u> and <u>marriage</u> are usually <u>positive</u> things — but Shakespeare uses the feud to show how strong feelings like <u>love</u> and <u>honour</u> can sometimes lead to <u>conflict</u>.

Ah, nothing like a good family feud...

All the lies Juliet tells are covering up the fact that she's married to a Montague. She knows what the rules are, and she'd rather not break them — but she has to because she's so in love. Aaaugh... urgh... ahem, sorry. I mean 'aww'...

Conflict, Honour and Feuds

When Romeo and Juliet fall in love it seems they can escape the feud, but that little delusion doesn't last...

Everyone Cares about Honour

1) The characters in *Romeo and Juliet* have a strong sense of <u>honour</u>.

2) Shakespeare shows that they're <u>easily drawn</u> into duels as they find it difficult to ignore <u>insults</u>. If someone insults them, they feel that their <u>family</u> and <u>friends</u> have also been insulted — so they've got to defend the <u>family honour</u>.

3) The feud is causing violence and <u>deaths</u>. But the Capulets and Montagues don't give up the feud — this shows that <u>honour</u> is more <u>important</u> to them than saving <u>lives</u>.

© Moviestore Collection Ltd

No one can Escape the Feud

1) The feud reveals some of the <u>major flaws</u> in the <u>social structure</u> of Verona:

- <u>Peaceful</u> people like Benvolio are <u>forced to fight</u> because of the importance of <u>family honour</u>.
- The <u>Prince</u> doesn't properly control the violence amongst the <u>upper classes</u>. He admits that he's been "<u>winking</u>" at their "<u>discords</u>" — maybe because they're <u>rich</u> and he wants to keep them happy.
- <u>Young</u>, <u>innocent</u> people such as Romeo and Juliet are forced to do <u>extreme things</u> to avoid the feud.

2) The feud <u>affects everything</u> that happens in the <u>plot</u>. Most of the <u>decisions</u> and <u>actions</u> made by the characters are <u>influenced</u> by the feud in one way or another.

Death and Violence The <u>violence</u> of the feud gradually gets <u>worse</u> through the play — it begins with a <u>street brawl</u> and ends in a <u>double suicide</u>. This creates <u>tension</u> as the audience wonders who'll be hurt next.

<u>Death</u> is seen as the only way to <u>escape</u> the feud. Whenever the feud keeps Romeo and Juliet apart, they threaten to <u>kill themselves</u>. In the end, the feud only <u>stops</u> because of their <u>deaths</u>.

Romeo and Juliet are Taking a Huge Risk...

1) The <u>feud</u> makes it feel as if everything is against them. Juliet tells Romeo that her family "<u>will murder</u>" him — so it's <u>dangerous</u> for them to be together and they have to get married in <u>secret</u>.

2) They're prepared to struggle against the odds — so in a way the <u>feud</u> makes their love seem even <u>stronger</u>.

3) The <u>visual contrast</u> between the <u>angry</u> fighting scenes and the <u>romantic</u> scenes also makes the love between Romeo and Juliet seem more <u>touching</u> and <u>beautiful</u>.

4) There's hope that their love will somehow be <u>stronger</u> than the feud. Friar Lawrence agrees to marry Romeo and Juliet because he hopes it will turn their "households' <u>rancour</u> to <u>pure love</u>".

5) As it turns out, their relationship <u>does</u> end the feud — but only after a lot of <u>bloodshed</u> and <u>tragedy</u>.

Hungry for a fight — must have more feud...

The feud crops up everywhere — it's central to the plot. Even if your essay's not specifically about the feud, at least give it a mention. If you leave it out, you're kind of missing the point.

Love

Here's another cheery page about love, death and madness. But mostly it's about love. It's tricky stuff, and one of the biggest themes of the play, so go and get a nice cup of tea before you start.

Romeo and Juliet's Love is the most *Important Thing* in the play

1) Romeo and Juliet fall in love at <u>first sight</u> — it's <u>powerful</u>, <u>exciting</u> and <u>dramatic</u>.

2) It's also supposed to be <u>true love</u> — <u>genuine</u> and <u>touching</u>, not just <u>teenage hormones</u> gone mad.

3) But Juliet is thirteen — so although it might be <u>true love</u>, it's also <u>young love</u>. Young love is traditionally seen as <u>headstrong</u> and <u>passionate</u>, not wise or realistic.

4) Shakespeare <u>deliberately</u> made Juliet this young. Maybe Juliet's age shows that the relationship was <u>immature</u> and <u>reckless</u>. Or perhaps it makes their actions seem even <u>braver</u>. It definitely makes the relationship <u>unconventional</u> and <u>striking</u>.

5) You could argue that their love is <u>destructive</u> — they put each others' <u>lives</u> in <u>danger</u>. If they hadn't treated love as the <u>only thing</u> worth <u>living</u> for, they wouldn't have died.

Shakespeare includes examples of *Courtly Love*

1) Romeo's relationship with <u>Rosaline</u> follows the traditions of <u>courtly love</u>. He won't stop loving her even though she wants to "<u>live chaste</u>" — she's not interested in him, so he ends up in "<u>despair</u>".

2) Mercutio <u>makes fun</u> of the way Romeo sighs and will "<u>Cry but 'Ay me!'</u>" This shows that courtly love was slightly <u>ridiculous</u> and <u>unrealistic</u>.

3) This <u>contrasts</u> with Romeo's <u>real love</u> for Juliet. He thinks he's in love with Rosaline — but finds out he's wrong when he meets Juliet. Romeo and Juliet's love is full of <u>emotion</u> and <u>passion</u>.

> <u>Courtly Love</u> was a way of <u>wooing</u> a lady in medieval times. The man <u>worshipped</u> her from afar, writing <u>poetry</u> and <u>songs</u> about the <u>perfection</u> of his <u>beloved</u>. The woman was often supposed to remain <u>cold</u> and <u>distant</u>, at least at first.

Mercutio and the *Nurse* often mention *Sexual Love*

© Photos 12 / Alamy

1) The <u>humorous</u> references to <u>physical desire</u> contrast with Romeo and Juliet's emotional <u>love</u> and commitment.

2) The servants make coarse jokes about "<u>my naked weapon</u>" and Mercutio jokes about Rosaline's "<u>quivering thigh</u>".

3) Shakespeare shows that Romeo and Juliet <u>desire</u>, as well as <u>love</u> each other. Romeo talks about the "<u>dear encounter</u>" of the wedding, and Juliet wants him to "<u>Leap to these arms</u>".

4) This makes their relationship more <u>convincing</u> — it is not just love <u>poetry</u> and <u>unrealistic romance</u> — there's <u>sex</u> too.

Shall I compare examiners to a summer's day...

Pssst... the goose flies at ten. In your essays, don't just describe the language Mr S. uses. Give your own interpretation or ideas about what effect he wants to have on the audience. She will lay her egg at midnight.

Fate

Fate — as in doom and destiny. Not the village fête, with a raffle and Mrs Hill's prize-winning marmalade...

Romeo and Juliet Look **Doomed** from the **Start**

It's nice to think we <u>control</u> our lives, but in bits of *Romeo and Juliet* Shakespeare suggests it's all down to fate.

1) <u>Right at the start</u> of the play, the Prologue says that Romeo and Juliet are <u>doomed</u> to die:

Key Quote

"From forth the fatal loins of these two foes
A pair of star-cross'd lovers take their life"
Prologue

© Moviestore Collection Ltd

2) The Prologue says the <u>stars</u> control Romeo and Juliet's lives, and the stars are <u>against</u> them. It's a bit like horoscopes — believing you can predict what will happen in the pattern of the stars.

3) There are references to <u>death</u> and <u>graves</u> and <u>curses</u> throughout the play — the audience is never allowed to forget that Romeo and Juliet are <u>doomed</u>.

4) The characters also <u>blame fate</u> and think they're <u>cursed</u>. As he's about to die, Romeo says he wants to "<u>shake the yoke of inauspicious stars</u>" — he wants to be free from his <u>fate</u>.

5) But fate's also a very <u>convenient idea</u> for Romeo at this point — it means it's <u>not</u> his fault Juliet died.

If You **Can't Blame Fate** What **Can** You Blame...

1) The characters use the <u>idea</u> of fate to <u>blame someone else</u> for the mess they're in. However, it's not clear if Romeo and Juliet were <u>destined</u> to have a tragic end, or if it all could've been <u>avoided</u>.

2) Perhaps <u>Romeo</u> and <u>Juliet</u> are responsible and it was all because of their <u>actions</u>. Or maybe the actions and choices of <u>other characters</u> are to blame. Or maybe it was a <u>combination</u> of personal responsibility <u>and</u> bad luck.

3) Shakespeare explores the idea of <u>fate versus personal responsibility</u> throughout *Romeo and Juliet*, and includes loads of <u>possible reasons</u> for why things went wrong — there's more than just <u>one</u> answer.

4) You could say they died <u>because</u>...

<u>Friar Lawrence</u> suggested a very dangerous plan — he didn't think through the possible risks.	<u>Romeo and Juliet</u> were too in love to think straight. They should have taken things more slowly.	The <u>feud</u> means that everything that happens in Verona ends in violence.
The <u>Nurse</u> didn't stop Juliet from getting involved with a Montague, or back her up when she said she wouldn't marry Paris.	<u>Juliet's parents</u> didn't pay enough attention to what Juliet felt or wanted.	It was all just <u>bad luck</u> and <u>bad timing</u>.

This is just a short list of reasons — think about all the possibilities and work out a combination you think makes sense.

Romeo and Juliet — it was fatal attraction...

When you write about themes, you can say pretty much whatever you want in your essays — but only if you back up everything you say with quotes, evidence and examples from the play, you lucky old thing, you.

Practice Questions

All this stuff on the context and themes explored in the play isn't just for a laugh, you know. If you can write about <u>why</u> Shakespeare uses religious imagery, or <u>how</u> different characters feel about love and desire, then you'll show you really understand the play. And you know what that means... better essays... more marks. Answer these questions as many times as it takes to make sure you've got all the information stored.

Quick Questions

1) Give two examples of ways in which religion was powerful in Shakespeare's time.

2) Why do Romeo and Juliet trust Friar Lawrence?

3) Were most marriages between rich people for love or for money in the 16th century?

4) Why is it dangerous for Romeo and Juliet to get married?

5) How does Shakespeare show that Romeo's love for Rosaline is probably courtly love?

6) How does the audience know that the play won't have a happy ending?

In-depth Questions

1) Describe one relationship of hate between characters in the play which contrasts with the relationship of love between Romeo and Juliet.

2) Does the help Friar Lawrence gives Romeo and Juliet fit in with his religious role?

3) Can Romeo avoid the violence of the feud? Why / why not?

4) What do you think about the play's portrayal of love? Is it always positive? Is it always realistic?

5) How does Shakespeare show that the family is important in *Romeo and Juliet*?

6) Use examples to show how Benvolio and Tybalt feel about the feud.

7) How important is the role of fate in the plot of Romeo and Juliet?

8) Why do you think Capulet reacts so violently when Juliet refuses to marry Paris?

Practice Questions

Context and Themes — it's one heck of a section. But you've gotta think whether you really know this stuff, because if you don't — buy my complete Knowledge Recall and Assimilation Pack for only £2000 plus p&p. Or alternatively, use the questions below to check you know the stuff.

Exam-Style Questions

1   a)   Discuss how the hatred and violence of the feud are presented in the passage below.

     b)   Discuss how the hatred and violence of the feud are presented at a different point in the play.

Sampson:	Draw if you be men. Gregory, remember thy washing blow. *They fight*
Benvolio:	Part, fools, put up your swords, you know not what you do.
	Enter Tybalt
Tybalt:	What, are thou drawn among these heartless hinds? Turn thee, Benvolio, look upon thy death.
Benvolio:	I do but keep the peace, put up thy sword, Or manage it to part these men with me.
Tybalt:	What, drawn, and talk of peace? I hate the word, As I hate hell, all Montagues, and thee: Have at thee, coward. *They fight*
	Enter three or four Citizens with clubs or partisans.
Citizens:	Clubs, bills and partisans! Strike! Beat them down! Down with the Capulets! Down with the Montagues!
	Enter old Capulet in his gown, and Lady Capulet.
Capulet:	What noise is this? Give me my long sword, ho!
Lady Cap.:	A crutch, a crutch! Why call you for a sword?
	Enter old Montague and Lady Montague
Capulet:	My sword I say! Old Montague is come, And flourishes his blade in spite of me.
Montague:	Thou villain Capulet! Hold me not! Let me go!
Lady Mon.:	Thou shalt not stir one foot to seek a foe.
	(Act 1, Scene 1)

Controlled Assessment-Style Questions

1   How are ideas of fate and free will presented in *Romeo and Juliet*?

2   Discuss how religion affects the relationship between Romeo and Juliet.

3   How does Shakespeare explore ideas of love and desire in *Romeo and Juliet*?

With some exam boards, you might have to <u>compare</u> the play with <u>another</u> text in your controlled assessment. These practice questions are still useful — just remember to discuss <u>two texts</u> in your answer.

Performing 'Romeo and Juliet'

Writing a play isn't like writing a novel — making the words work on paper isn't enough. Stagecraft is the skill of writing a play so that it works on stage. Shakespeare's stagecraft was the cat's bananas.

Stagecraft is **Play-Writing Skill**

©Tony Larkin/Rex Features

1) Stagecraft is all the things that playwrights do to make a play fantastic when it's <u>performed</u> on stage.

2) Elizabethan theatres <u>didn't bother</u> with backdrops or fancy sets — so the <u>words</u> in the script were important for <u>setting the scene</u> and creating <u>different moods</u> as well as telling the story.

3) If you see *Romeo and Juliet* performed, you should find it's <u>moving</u>, dramatic and <u>keeps you hooked</u> right to the end. All that's down to <u>how</u> Shakespeare chose to tell the story.

A play's **Structure** is the **Way** it's **Put Together**

1) One of the most important parts of stagecraft is the <u>structure</u> of the play. The structure is the <u>overall design</u> of the play — how the <u>plot</u> is revealed, what <u>events</u> happen when, which scenes focus on <u>thoughts</u> and <u>feelings</u>, and which scenes build towards a <u>dramatic climax</u>.

2) Shakespeare didn't just put the scenes in a <u>random order</u> — he had <u>reasons</u> to structure them a <u>certain way</u>:

To Emphasise Important Themes	**To Control or Change the Mood of the Play**
He puts a <u>fight</u> between the two families right at the <u>beginning</u> in Act 1, Scene 1. That way the audience are immediately shown how <u>violent</u> the <u>feud</u> is.	He put most of the <u>comic scenes</u> in the <u>first</u> half of the play, and the <u>tragic</u> and suspenseful scenes towards the <u>end</u>. That way it <u>doesn't seem odd</u> having comic bits in a tragic play.

Shakespeare **Varies** the **Lengths** of the **Scenes**

1) Some scenes need to be <u>long</u> — to properly <u>develop</u> key events and <u>explore</u> characters' feelings.

- For example, the <u>balcony scene</u> in Act 2 is the <u>only</u> scene where Romeo and Juliet are alone for more than a few minutes. After watching this scene the audience has to be <u>convinced</u> that they really, really <u>love</u> each other — the rest of the plot is silly otherwise.

2) Putting <u>short</u> scenes in between long ones changes the <u>mood</u>. Things happen <u>faster</u>, so it's more <u>exciting</u>.

- In Act 5, there are two little scenes where Romeo finds out <u>Juliet's dead</u> and Friar Lawrence finds out the <u>letter hasn't arrived</u>. These are the last pieces of the <u>tragedy</u> slotting into place. Making them short gives the audience the impression of everything <u>hurtling out of control</u>.

Stagecraft — ships that prompt in the night...

Shakespeare didn't want people getting bored — or finding the lovey and tragic bits funny.
He had to use every trick he knew to make the audience laugh, cry and give him their money.

The Structure of 'Romeo and Juliet'

Romeo and Juliet is made up of key scenes and minor scenes. It's not full-on romance and tragedy all the way through — but every bit is there for a reason and scenes can have lots of different purposes.

The **First Half** is structured around the **Growing Romance**

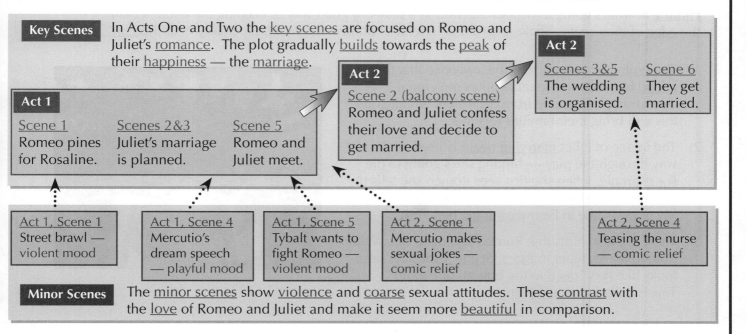

Key Scenes
In Acts One and Two the key scenes are focused on Romeo and Juliet's romance. The plot gradually builds towards the peak of their happiness — the marriage.

Act 1
Scene 1
Romeo pines for Rosaline.

Scenes 2&3
Juliet's marriage is planned.

Scene 5
Romeo and Juliet meet.

Act 2
Scene 2 (balcony scene)
Romeo and Juliet confess their love and decide to get married.

Act 2
Scenes 3&5
The wedding is organised.

Scene 6
They get married.

Act 1, Scene 1
Street brawl — violent mood

Act 1, Scene 4
Mercutio's dream speech — playful mood

Act 1, Scene 5
Tybalt wants to fight Romeo — violent mood

Act 2, Scene 1
Mercutio makes sexual jokes — comic relief

Act 2, Scene 4
Teasing the nurse — comic relief

Minor Scenes
The minor scenes show violence and coarse sexual attitudes. These contrast with the love of Romeo and Juliet and make it seem more beautiful in comparison.

In the **Second Half**, events **Accelerate** towards **Tragedy**

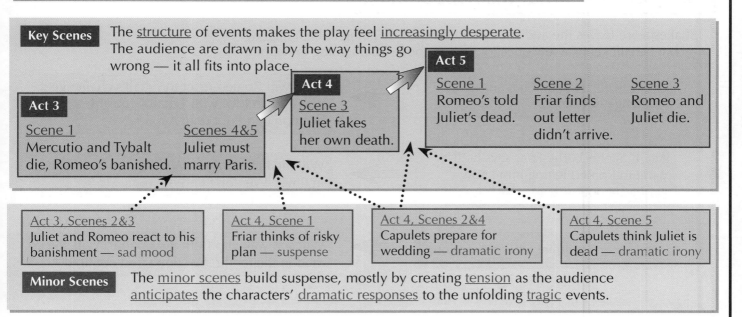

Key Scenes
The structure of events makes the play feel increasingly desperate. The audience are drawn in by the way things go wrong — it all fits into place.

Act 3
Scene 1
Mercutio and Tybalt die, Romeo's banished.

Scenes 4&5
Juliet must marry Paris.

Act 4
Scene 3
Juliet fakes her own death.

Act 5
Scene 1
Romeo's told Juliet's dead.

Scene 2
Friar finds out letter didn't arrive.

Scene 3
Romeo and Juliet die.

Act 3, Scenes 2&3
Juliet and Romeo react to his banishment — sad mood

Act 4, Scene 1
Friar thinks of risky plan — suspense

Act 4, Scenes 2&4
Capulets prepare for wedding — dramatic irony

Act 4, Scene 5
Capulets think Juliet is dead — dramatic irony

Minor Scenes
The minor scenes build suspense, mostly by creating tension as the audience anticipates the characters' dramatic responses to the unfolding tragic events.

Romeo, is that a banana in your pocket or just our growing romance...

If you're writing about structure, I'd suggest focusing on key scenes — the ones where romance and tragedy are at their peak. It's fine to discuss minor scenes too — but don't make them the main subject (unless the question mentions them).

The Structure of 'Romeo and Juliet'

Shakespeare knew how to keep the audience from yawning — hint that juicy scenes are coming up, without giving it all away. Easy.

Shakespeare **Prepares** you for what's **Going** to **Happen**

Hinting at what's going to happen later on in a play is a good way of keeping the audience on the edge of their seats. Shakespeare does it a lot in *Romeo and Juliet*, especially near the start.

©Everett Collection/Rex Features

1) The Prologue to Act 1 tells the audience that there's a feud between two great families in Verona. Two young lovers, one from each side, will die and this will bring their families together.

2) The image of Juliet marrying death is used all the way through the play — hinting she's going to die. For example, when she first sees Romeo she tells the Nurse: "Go ask his name. If he be marrièd, My grave is like to be my wedding bed."

3) There are also hints that Romeo's going to die. When Romeo leaves Juliet in Act 3, Scene 5 she says he looks like he's "dead in the bottom of a tomb". This is called foreshadowing.

Suspense — what will happen next?

Shakespeare leaves the audience in little doubt it's going to be a tragedy — but he still keeps a few questions open about what's going to happen.

Act 2, Scene 4 Tybalt has sent a challenge to Romeo.	How will Romeo react to Tybalt's challenge now he's in love with Tybalt's cousin? We don't find out until Act 3.
Act 4, Scene 1 The Friar says he'll write to Romeo letting him know about the potion.	Will the letter arrive? Will Romeo be warned in time? We don't find out until Act 5.
Act 4, Scene 3 Juliet takes the potion.	Will she wake up from the potion? Will she go mad in the tomb? We don't find out until Act 5.

Hold on Romeo — I'll never let go...

It's a bit like the stupid bit of your brain that hopes the ship won't hit the iceberg, even though you know it's going to. Some foolish brain cell starts going, "But maybe he'll realise she's alive, maybe it'll all be all right..."

Mood and Atmosphere

Shakespeare creates all sorts of different moods in *Romeo and Juliet*. This makes the play more interesting and keeps the audience hooked — they laugh, they cry, they bite their fingernails on the edge of their seats...

The **Mood Changes** throughout the **Play**...

1) The play <u>isn't</u> just death and <u>destruction</u> all the way through. It's easier for the audience to <u>care</u> about <u>characters</u> if they see them when they're <u>happy</u> first.

2) Shakespeare lets the audience know it's a tragedy in the <u>Prologue</u> to Act 1, and he keeps putting in little <u>reminders</u> that bad things are going to happen. Otherwise he keeps it <u>relatively light</u> in the first two acts. Romeo and Juliet meet, fall in love and get married.

3) Then <u>Act 3</u> starts with <u>violence</u> and <u>death</u>. The funniest character is killed and puts a curse on everyone. Romeo kills Juliet's cousin. From here on in, it gets pretty <u>bleak</u>.

Different Settings create different **Moods**

1) The play's set in <u>Verona</u>, in Northern Italy. However, there's nothing in the play that's <u>specifically Italian</u> — no Italian is spoken and there aren't any references to Italian <u>culture</u>.

2) The setting would've made it seem very <u>exotic</u> to Elizabethan audiences, perhaps making it <u>easier to imagine</u> such a dramatic story happening.

3) There are quite a few different settings within Verona, which help to create the right atmosphere for each scene, e.g.

> Romeo and Juliet meet at a <u>party</u> — so the atmosphere is <u>fun</u>.

> The <u>final scene</u> is set at <u>night</u> in a graveyard and <u>tomb</u>. It's a suitably <u>gloomy</u> and <u>morbid</u> setting for the <u>tragic ending</u>.

Shakespeare uses **Language** *to* **Create Atmosphere**

1) Sometimes what the characters <u>say</u> helps to <u>set the scene</u>. Using <u>dialogue</u> to describe the <u>setting</u> and <u>atmosphere</u> was particularly <u>important</u> in Shakespeare's time, because <u>sets</u> and <u>props</u> were limited.

2) For example, Benvolio's speech in Act 3 lets the audience know that it's the height of <u>summer</u>, the scene's set <u>outdoors</u> and the atmosphere is <u>violent</u>.

> "The day is hot, the Capels are abroad,
> And if we meet we shall not scape a brawl,
> For now, these hot days, is the mad blood stirring."
> Act 3, Scene 1

3) At other times, the <u>language</u> creates an <u>atmosphere</u> of its own — one that isn't linked to the setting, but more to do with what's going on in the <u>characters' minds</u>.

4) When she's about to drink the potion, Juliet talks about "<u>bloody Tybalt</u>" who is "<u>festering in his shroud</u>". This <u>death-fixated language</u> and <u>imagery</u> creates a really spooky, <u>morbid atmosphere</u>.

Nowadays we'd just use a dimmer switch...

... but there wasn't any mood lighting or Barry White back then — Shakespeare had to rely on his own wit and ready repartee to create atmosphere. I suppose he could've used candles, but then there'd be nothing to write essays about.

Dramatic Irony

There's a whole heap of dramatic irony in the play. The audience knows all about Romeo and Juliet's love and marriage, and their fate, but a lot of the characters on stage have no idea.

*Romeo and Juliet's **Parents** and **Friends** don't have a **Clue***

Dramatic irony is when the audience knows something that a character on stage doesn't know. It adds suspense — the audience knows the character's got it wrong and wonders what they'll do when they find out the truth.

1) Shakespeare lets the audience know what's happening to Romeo and Juliet. But some of the characters on stage don't know anything:

In Act 3, Mercutio doesn't know why Romeo won't fight Tybalt:

"O calm, dishonourable, vile submission"

 But the audience knows it's because Romeo's just married Tybalt's cousin, Juliet.

In Act 4, the Capulets happily prepare for Juliet's marriage to Paris:

"Make haste! The bridegroom he is come already."

 The audience knows that Juliet has taken the Friar's potion and the Capulets are going to get a horrible shock.

2) The effect of dramatic irony is to make the audience feel more involved with the story — they understand the true results of the characters' actions better than the characters do.

3) If the audience feels involved with the story, they're also more likely to respond emotionally.

*The **Friar's Potion** fools nearly everyone*

One of the most powerful uses of dramatic irony in *Romeo and Juliet* is Juliet's fake death.

1) Juliet doesn't tell the Nurse about the potion plan. When she finds Juliet in Act 4, her grief is very moving — but the audience also knows that she's been deceived.

2) Romeo doesn't get the letter — so he also believes that Juliet's dead. The audience knows she's alive but can also see that her supposed death is causing Romeo to commit suicide.

3) This keeps the audience in suspense — they keep hoping Juliet will wake up in time, and it's very emotional watching Romeo commit suicide, knowing that it's completely unnecessary.

© AF archive / Alamy

Theme — Fate

The audience knows that Romeo and Juliet are "star-cross'd" from the start. Every time the characters mention "fortune" or "fate", it reminds the audience that the characters are headed for death and despair.

Ironing whilst sky-diving — now that's dramatic...

You can try shouting "Don't do it Romeo, she's alive, she's alive!" — but the actor probably won't pay any attention to you. You might even be asked to leave the theatre — the snooty so-and-sos. Still, that's dramatic irony for you...

Poetry in Shakespeare

This page is a bit dull and technical, but I haven't just stuck it in to wind you up.
If you know the rules about the poetry, it'll be easier to read and easier to write about. Sigh.

Shakespeare *Mainly* uses **Blank Verse**

1) Blank verse is a type of poetry that follows these <u>three rules</u>:

- The lines usually <u>don't rhyme</u>.
- Each line has <u>10</u> or <u>11</u> syllables.
- Each line has <u>5</u> big beats.

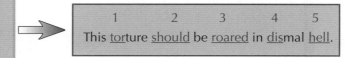

1	2	3	4	5

This <u>torture</u> <u>should</u> be <u>roared</u> in <u>dismal</u> <u>hell</u>.

2) Even in short, choppy bits of <u>conversation</u> Shakespeare usually sticks to five big beats a line. The words are <u>staggered</u> to show that they're all part of <u>one line</u> of poetry:

	1	2	3	4	5
TYBALT: I'll <u>not</u> en<u>dure</u> him.
CAPULET: <u>He</u> shall <u>be</u> en<u>dur'd</u>.

3) For <u>serious</u> and <u>important</u> bits the rhythm is <u>regular</u>. The Prince and other <u>upper-class</u> characters nearly always talk in this <u>regular</u> rhythm — it makes them sound <u>posh</u>:

1	2	3	4	5

Once <u>more</u>, on <u>pain</u> of <u>death</u>, all <u>men</u> de<u>part</u>.

4) More <u>lower-class</u> characters, like the <u>Nurse</u> and <u>servants</u>, often talk in <u>prose</u> and without much <u>set rhythm</u>.

Some of the poetry **Rhymes**

1) Some scenes have <u>bits</u> of rhyme in. Rhymes are used to <u>emphasise</u> when two people <u>agree</u>:

Juliet: O now be gone, more light and light it **grows**.
Romeo: More light and light, more dark and dark our **woes**.
Act 3, Scene 5

© Moviestore Collection Ltd

2) Rhymes are also used to make two lines of speech sound more <u>final</u> or to <u>emphasise</u> that it's <u>important</u>:

For never was a story of more **woe**
Than this of Juliet and her **Romeo**.
Act 5, Scene 3

A **Sonnet** is an **Important** type of **Poetry**

1) A <u>sonnet</u> has <u>fourteen lines</u>, and usually a strict rhyme scheme.

2) During Shakespeare's time, a lot of <u>love poetry</u> was written in <u>sonnet form</u> — so sonnets would've reminded the audience of <u>romance</u> and <u>love</u>.

Some Important Sonnets in *Romeo and Juliet*:

- the <u>Prologues</u> at the beginnings of Acts 1 and 2
- the <u>first</u> fourteen lines Romeo and Juliet say to <u>each other</u> in Act 1, Scene 5

Poetry in Shakespeare

Shakespeare Changes the Pace

1) <u>Long</u> words and sentences s l o w   t h i n g s   d o w n.
   For example, in this bit Juliet sounds <u>thoughtful</u> and <u>dreamy</u>.

> "Lovers can see to do their amorous rites
> By their own beauties, or if love be blind,
> It best agrees with night."
> Act 3, Scene 2

> "Look to't, think on't, I do not use to jest.
> Thursday is near. Lay hand on heart. Advise."
> Act 3, Scene 5

2) <u>Short</u> words and sentences <u>speed things up</u>. Here it's been used to make Capulet sound <u>angry</u>.

Different Rhythms are used to show Different Emotions

1) Shakespeare often changes the rhythm of lines by messing around with <u>punctuation</u> and choice of <u>words</u>.

2) This bit's got a <u>steady rhythm</u>.
   The Friar's asked him to calm down, so Romeo's trying to be <u>controlled</u> and reasonable.

> "Then plainly know my heart's dear love is set
> On the fair daughter of rich Capulet."
> Act 2, Scene 3

3) Here, the punctuation's very <u>choppy</u>. The rhythm's all over the place. Mercutio's just been stabbed and knows he is dying — the rhythm shows that he's in a lot of <u>pain</u> and very <u>angry</u>.

> "They have made worms' meat of me.
> I have it, and soundly too. Your houses!"
> Act 3, Scene 1

Word Order Emphasises different words

1) Sometimes the word order changes to make <u>important</u> words <u>stand out</u> more.

> "**Poison**, I see, hath been his timeless end."
> Act 5, Scene 3

2) The <u>natural</u> way to say this would be:
   "I see poison hath been his timeless end."

3) But if "<u>Poison</u>" is at the start then it gets more <u>emphasis</u>.

A Soliloquy shows the Character's Thoughts and Feelings

1) A <u>soliloquy</u> is a long speech by <u>one character</u> that is not spoken to any other character on stage.

2) It's just them <u>thinking out loud</u> about their <u>emotions</u>, so it's a good way of showing the audience how a character is honestly feeling.

Some Important Soliloquies in *Romeo and Juliet*:

• Juliet's speech on her balcony in Act 2, Scene 2.

• Romeo's speech before he drinks poison, in Act 5, Scene 3.

© AF archive / Alamy

Shakespeare was a poet — but did he know it...

Don't just describe what poetry is used — always write about how Shakespeare uses poetry to create different effects.

Puns and Wordplay

Romeo and Juliet is full of puns. Some of them are meant to be funny, but they're not hilarious.

There are **Puns** Everywhere

1) Shakespeare loved puns — his plays are <u>full</u> of them.
They were really <u>popular</u> at the time he was writing.

2) Sometimes they're meant to be <u>funny</u>, and sometimes it's just <u>clever wordplay</u>.

> SAMSON: I mean, and we be in **choler**, we'll **draw**.
> GREGORY: Ay, while you live, **draw** your neck out of **collar**.
> Act 1, Scene 1

This means "if we're angry, we'll draw our swords".

But this means "keep your head out of a noose" i.e. a hangman's "collar".

3) Gregory's making a <u>pun</u> on the words "choler" (<u>anger</u>) and "collar" (<u>noose</u>).

4) Choler and collar are <u>pronounced</u> the same (they're <u>homophones</u>), so to the <u>audience</u> they would sound like the <u>same word</u>.

Some **Puns** are part of an **Image**

1) At the end of the play, Montague promises to put up a <u>gold statue</u> of Juliet:

> "There shall no **figure** at such **rate** be set
> As that of true and faithful Juliet."
> Act 5, Scene 3

2) He's making puns on the words "<u>figure</u>" and "<u>rate</u>" — the sentence means "no person will be respected so highly as Juliet", but it also means "no statue will be worth so much money as Juliet's". It's about <u>money</u> as well as <u>love</u>.

This 'gold' statue of Juliet is actually in Verona — it's a popular tourist attraction.

Mercutio's speech is **Full** of **Puns**

1) <u>Mercutio</u> makes puns all the time — <u>even</u> when he's dying:

> Ask for me tomorrow, and you shall find me a **grave** man.
> Act 3, Scene 1

2) He's making a pun about "grave" meaning <u>serious</u>, and the "grave" he'll be <u>buried in</u> tomorrow.

3) It's a really <u>bitter joke</u> — instead of being funny, it's incredibly <u>sad</u>.

A play on words — Romeo & Juliet do a crossword...
Romeo and Juliet is full of puns. Shakespeare thought they were really punny. You might not, but remember that an Elizabethan audience would probably have found them hilarious. Maybe not the death ones.

Imagery and Symbolism

Romeo and Juliet is full of images — they make the language rich and interesting, and help the audience understand the thoughts and feelings of the characters. Of course, they also make the play a bit tricky to study.

There are **Three Kinds** of **Formal Imagery** to **Look Out For**

Imagery is when things are described in a really vivid way. But there are three types of imagery that are a bit more complicated. You need to know how to recognise these — it'll impress the examiners no end.

Similes are when **One** thing is **Like Something** else

> "But old folks, many feign as they were dead,
> Unwieldy, slow, heavy, and **pale as lead**."
> Act 2, Scene 5

1) This one's saying old people are pale, like lead. Lead isn't exactly "slow", but it is unwieldy (awkward to carry) and heavy too.

2) Epic similes are extra-long similes. These images have a lot of impact — they give the audience more time and detail to help them form a picture in their minds.

3) In this epic simile, Juliet's comparing her love to the sea — the whole thing is about the same image.

> "My bounty is as **boundless as the sea,**
> **My love as deep; the more I give to thee**
> **The more I have, for both are infinite.**"
> Act 2, Scene 2

A Metaphor is when **One** thing is said to be **Something Else**

1) Here, Romeo says Juliet has wounded him, and he's wounded Juliet.

> "Where on a sudden one hath **wounded** me,
> That's by me **wounded**"
> Act 2, Scene 3

2) This doesn't mean Romeo's actually been hurt — it means Romeo has fallen in love and it feels like he's been wounded.

© Pictorial Press Ltd / Alamy

Personification means **Describing** a thing **As If** it were a **Person**

> "Now **old desire** does in his deathbed lie,
> And **young affection** gapes to be his heir"
> Act 2, Prologue

Here "old desire" for Rosaline is described as a dying old man. "Young affection" (for Juliet) is described like a greedy son, waiting for his father to die so he can take his place.

Shakespeare's images — homeboy bard, punk bard...

Learn all the three types of imagery, and use them in your essays. Maybe even drop them into everyday conversations — that'll be sure to impress. Mind you, arriving at school by abseiling from a helicopter would be more impressive.

Imagery and Symbolism

The main point of imagery is to liven up the language, and make the themes more obvious.

Light Symbolises Romeo and Juliet's Love for each other...

1) <u>Romeo</u> describes <u>Juliet</u> as a <u>light</u> in <u>darkness</u>. It makes Juliet sound <u>beautiful</u>, and shows how to Romeo she <u>stands out</u> from everything else.

Images of Light...

"O she doth teach the torches to burn bright!"
Act 1, Scene 5

"But soft, what light through yonder window breaks?
It is the east, and Juliet is the sun."
Act 2, Scene 2

Juliet's so beautiful that she seems to shine more brightly than the torches that light the party.

It's night-time — to Romeo, seeing Juliet is like looking at the dawn.

2) <u>Juliet</u> uses an image of <u>lightning</u> to describe their love, saying it is "too <u>sudden</u>, / too like the <u>lightning</u>, which doth cease to be".

3) This image uses light to show a <u>different side</u> to their love — it will be <u>powerful</u> and <u>shocking</u>, but may only last for a <u>little while</u>.

Theme — Conflict

The bitter strength of the <u>feud</u> mean that Romeo and Juliet live in a <u>dark</u>, <u>violent</u> society. Using images of light shows how their love <u>lights up</u> that darkness and offers hope of <u>ending</u> the feud.

... But their Relationship is full of Images of Darkness

1) Although <u>light</u> symbolises their love, Shakespeare uses <u>images of darkness</u> to remind the audience that it is a <u>doomed</u> relationship.

2) Because it's all a <u>secret</u>, they can only be <u>together</u> when there's "<u>night's cloak to hide</u>" them.

3) This <u>need for darkness</u> is shown when Juliet pretends "It was the <u>nightingale</u> and <u>not</u> the <u>lark</u>" because she doesn't want it to be morning.

4) At the end, the sun "will <u>not show</u> his head" — darkness has <u>triumphed</u> and the light of their love's <u>died</u>.

© Moviestore Collection Ltd

Their Love is sometimes Described using Religious Imagery

1) Romeo and Juliet's conversations are full of images of <u>angels</u>, <u>saints</u> and <u>gods</u>.

2) These images could show that their love is <u>pure</u> and <u>innocent</u> — <u>approved</u> by God.

3) Or it might suggest that their love is <u>out of control</u> — they don't just love each other, they worship each other.

4) This could be seen as dangerous and sinful — you weren't supposed to worship anyone <u>except</u> God.

Religious Imagery

"My lips, two blushing pilgrims, ready stand"
Act 1, Scene 5

"swear by thy gracious self,
Which is the god of my idolatry"
Act 2, Scene 2

Section Five — Shakespeare's Techniques

54

Imagery and Symbolism

Images of *Time* and *Speed* make everything feel **Rushed**

1) Time imagery makes Romeo and Juliet sound impatient — it seems as if they're trying to speed everything up because it feels too slow.

2) Romeo says "sad hours seem long" and Juliet says "tomorrow! 'Tis twenty year till then" — their feelings make time seem to drag slowly.

3) But for the audience, everything is rushed because loads of big events happen in a short space of time.

Theme — Love

Shakespeare explores ideas of love and time. He uses images of time to suggest that their love is too rushed. But he also uses time to show that it's an incredibly powerful love: Romeo is overwhelmed by "the exchange of joy / that one short minute" gives when he's with her.

© PARAMOUNT / THE KOBAL COLLECTION

Shakespeare uses **Time Imagery** to create **Suspense**...

1) The Friar repeatedly warns Romeo and Juliet that they shouldn't rush because "they stumble that run fast".

2) With repeated warnings, Shakespeare is hinting to the audience that something bad is going to happen, but it increases the tension as they don't know when or how.

3) Other things happen to show that bad timing is going to affect the tragedy:

- Benvolio describes Mercutio's death as "too untimely".
- Capulet asks Paris "Do you like this haste?" as he arranges his daughter's marriage for three days' time.

... and **Natural Imagery** to **Describe** the **Characters**

1) Shakespeare uses sea images to show that the characters get swept away by powerful emotions.

2) Juliet's body is described as a boat tossed around by her emotions, and her sighs are like the wind.

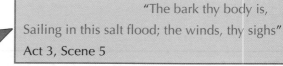
"The bark thy body is, Sailing in this salt flood; the winds, thy sighs" Act 3, Scene 5

3) Flower images show that Juliet's a beautiful, romantic heroine, because they're linked to love and beauty.

4) Here, it's also a sad contrast — flowers are bright and full of life and energy, but Juliet has died.

"Sweet flower, with flowers thy bridal bed I strew" Act 5, Scene 3

Who says poetry isn't wet and flowery...

Shakespeare used loads of images for all sorts of reasons, so if your essay's on his use of language make sure you write shedloads on it. In fact, imagery needs at least a mention in most types of essay — go on, you know you want to...

Practice Questions

You need to get Shakespeare's techniques sorted out. It's one of the things the examiners expect you to understand. It's all about how Shakespeare made the play good — well-told, atmospheric, gripping... And the key to a lot of those things is <u>structure</u>. So answer these questions, and keep going through them until you know the answers. Then you can pass the exam, get a job, become a reality TV star, whatever...

Quick Questions

1) Why does Shakespeare vary the length of the scenes?

2) How and when does Shakespeare let the audience know that the play will end in tragedy?

3) Find two scenes where the mood is:
   a) romantic   b) tragic

4) Describe one example of dramatic irony that Shakespeare uses in *Romeo and Juliet*.

5) How many lines are there in a sonnet?

6) "How silver-sweet sound lovers' tongues by night / like softest music to attending ears."

   Is this...   a) a simile   b) a metaphor   c) personification

In-depth Questions

1) Pick a scene in the play and describe how it helps build tension and suspense.

2) Pick a scene in the play and describe how it helps give the audience a bit of comic relief.

3) What is dramatic irony? Why do you think Shakespeare uses it in *Romeo and Juliet*?

4) Explain how Shakespeare uses language and poetic structures to make the balcony scene romantic.

5) Find an epic simile in the play. Explain what the imagery shows us, and how it fits with the atmosphere of the rest of the scene.

6) Why do you think Shakespeare gives the Nurse a lot of puns in her speech?

7) a) Which of these themes and emotions are sometimes emphasised using images of light?

   i) love   ii) fate   iii) conflict   iv) sadness   v) anger   vi) desire

   b) Why do you think Shakespeare uses so many images of light in *Romeo and Juliet*?

Practice Questions

Well, enough of that easy-peasy warm-up stuff. Now it's time to show off your sparkling skills of analysis, insight and general fabulousness with these exam-style questions. Enjoy...

Exam-Style Questions

1 a) Discuss how Shakespeare shows the developing relationship between Romeo and Juliet in the passage below. Remember to write about:
   - the thoughts and feelings in the passage.
   - the techniques Shakespeare uses to show the developing relationship between Romeo and Juliet in the passage.

> **Romeo**: If I profane with my unworthiest hand
> This holy shrine, the gentle sin is this:
> My lips, two blushing pilgrims ready stand
> To smooth that rough touch with a tender kiss.
>
> **Juliet**: Good pilgrim, you do wrong your hand too much,
> Which mannerly devotion shows in this;
> For saints have hands that pilgrims' hands do touch,
> And palm to palm is holy palmers' kiss.
>
> **Romeo**: Have not saints lips, and holy palmers too?
>
> **Juliet**: Ay, pilgrim, lips that they must use in prayer.
>
> **Romeo**: O then, dear saint, let lips do what hands do:
> They pray: grant thou, lest faith turn to despair.
>
> **Juliet**: Saints do not move, though grant for prayer's sake.
>
> **Romeo**: Then move not, while my prayer's effect I take.
>
> *[He kisses her]*
>
> (Act 1, Scene 5, 92-105)

   b) Discuss the techniques Shakespeare uses in a different part of the play to show the relationship between Romeo and Juliet.

Controlled Assessment-Style Questions

1 Explore the methods Shakespeare uses to present different types of love in *Romeo and Juliet*.

2 Examine how Shakespeare uses language to present the character of Tybalt in *Romeo and Juliet*.

3 Look at the way Shakespeare presents conflict in *Romeo and Juliet*.

> With some exam boards, you might have to compare the play with another text in your controlled assessment. These practice questions are still useful — just remember to discuss two texts in your answer.

Assessment Advice — The Exam

These pages will help you write a <u>scorching exam answer</u>, more scorching than, say, Brad Pitt walking across a bed of hot coals to cook a curry. If you're studying the play for <u>Controlled Assessment</u>, these pages are still worth a look — they'll help you with your <u>essay structure</u>.

The exam questions will test **Three Main Skills**

Show the examiner that you can:

1) Write about the text in a <u>thoughtful way</u> with suitable <u>examples</u> and <u>quotations</u> to back up your points.

2) <u>Identify and explain</u> features of the play's <u>form</u>, <u>structure</u> and <u>language</u>. Show how Shakespeare uses these to present the <u>ideas</u>, <u>themes</u>, <u>characters</u> and <u>settings</u> effectively.

3) Write with good <u>spelling</u>, <u>grammar</u>, <u>punctuation</u> and <u>paragraphing</u> — it'll help you get the top marks.

Read the Question *Carefully* and *Underline Key Words*

1) In the exam, you'll usually get a <u>choice of two questions</u> and you'll have to <u>pick one</u>.

2) The question will have a <u>Part A</u> and a <u>Part B</u>. <u>Read</u> the whole question at least <u>twice</u>, so you completely understand it. <u>Underline</u> the key words.

Here's an exam-style question

Think about the <u>techniques</u> Shakespeare uses to get his point across. E.g. the <u>structure</u> of the <u>dialogue</u> and the <u>imagery</u>.

Think about what their <u>language</u> tells us about their <u>thoughts</u> and <u>feelings</u>.

Focus on the <u>extract</u> — <u>don't</u> discuss the rest of the play <u>yet</u>.

Q1 a) <u>How</u> does Shakespeare explore the <u>feelings</u> and the <u>relationship</u> between <u>Romeo and Friar Lawrence</u> in the <u>passage below</u>?

b) <u>How</u> does Shakespeare present <u>different aspects</u> of Romeo and the Friar's <u>relationship</u> in <u>another</u> part of the play?

Try to pick a bit of the play that shows a <u>different side</u> to their <u>relationship</u>. E.g. Act 3, Scene 3.

Friar L: If ere thou wast thyself, and these woes thine,
              Thou and these woes were all for Rosaline.
              And art thou chang'd? Pronounce this sentence then:
              Women may fall when there's no strength in men.
Romeo: Thou chid'st me oft for loving Rosaline.
Friar L: For doting, not for loving, pupil mine.
Romeo: And bad'st me bury love.
Friar L: Not in a grave
              To lay one in, another out to have.
Romeo: I pray thee chide me not, her I love now
              Doth grace for grace and love for love allow.
              The other did not so.
Friar L: O, she knew well
              Thy love did read by rote that could not spell.
              But come young waverer, come, go with me,
              In one respect I'll thy assistant be.
              For this alliance may so happy prove
              To turn your households' rancour to pure love.

The advice squad — the best cops in the NYPD...

Whatever question you're asked in the exam, your answer should touch on the main characters, themes, structure and language of the play. All the stuff we've covered in the rest of the book in fact. It's so neat, it's almost like we planned it.

Structure and Planning

It's easy to panic in the exam — all the more reason to spend 5 minutes jotting down a <u>cunning plan</u> for what you're going to write. It'll give you time to think and give your answer a better <u>structure</u>.

Plan your answer before you start

1) If you plan, you're less likely to forget something <u>important</u>.

2) Write your plan at the <u>top of your answer booklet</u> and draw a <u>neat line</u> through it when you've finished.

3) <u>Don't</u> spend <u>too long</u> on your plan. It's only <u>rough work</u>, so you don't need to write in full sentences. Here are a few <u>examples</u> of different ways you can plan your answer:

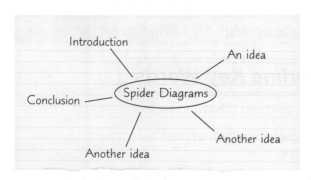

Bullet points and headings...
* Intro...
* An idea...
* The next idea...

Tables with...

A point...	Quote to back this up...
Another point...	Quote...
A different point...	Quote...
A brand new point...	Quote...

4) A good plan will help you <u>organise</u> your ideas — and write a good, <u>well-structured</u> essay.

Structure your answer

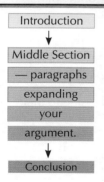

Introduction
↓
Middle Section
— paragraphs
expanding
your
argument.
↓
Conclusion

1) Your <u>introduction</u> should give a brief answer to the question you're writing about. Make it clear how you're going to <u>tackle the topic</u>.

2) The <u>middle section</u> of your essay should explain your answer in detail and give evidence to back it up. Write a <u>paragraph</u> for each point you make. Start the paragraph by making the <u>point</u>, then <u>back it up</u> with <u>evidence</u> — examples and quotations. Make sure you <u>comment</u> on your evidence and <u>explain how</u> it helps to <u>prove</u> your point.

3) Remember to write a <u>conclusion</u> — a paragraph at the end which <u>sums up</u> your <u>main points</u>.

Dirk finally felt ready to tackle the topic.

Don't Panic if you make a *Mistake*

1) Okay, so say the exam is going well and you've timed it beautifully. Instead of putting your feet up on the desk for the last 5 minutes, it's a good idea to <u>read through</u> your <u>answers</u> at the end and <u>correct any mistakes</u>...

2) If you want to get rid of something, just <u>cross it out</u>. <u>Don't scribble</u> over it.

3) If you've <u>left stuff out</u> write it in a separate section at the end of the essay. Put a <u>star</u> (*) next to both the extra <u>writing</u> and the <u>place</u> you want it to go.

To plan or not to plan, that is the question...
The answer is yes, yes, a thousand times yes. Often students dive right in, worried that planning will take up valuable time. But 5 minutes spent organising a well-structured answer is loads better than pages of waffle. Mmm waffles.

Sample Exam — Planning Part A

And now the bit you've all been waiting for — a lovely little sample plan for Part A of the question. Enjoy.

Have **Another Look** at the **Extract...**

Read the extract <u>closely</u> and underline the important bits.
Think about how they <u>talk</u>, the <u>layout</u> and <u>structure</u> of the dialogue, <u>rhyme</u> and <u>imagery</u>.

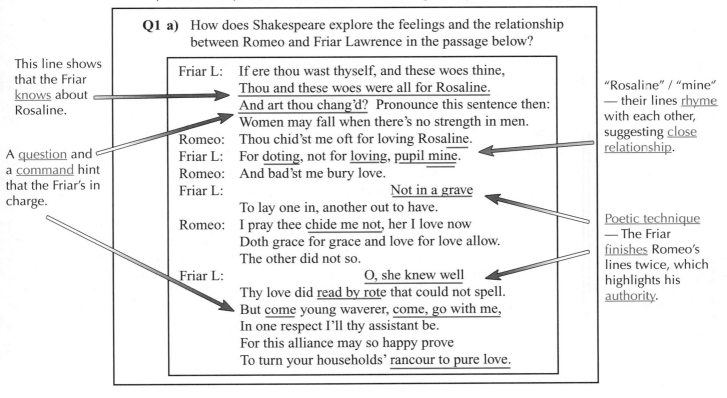

This line shows that the Friar <u>knows</u> about Rosaline.

A <u>question</u> and a <u>command</u> hint that the Friar's in charge.

Q1 a) How does Shakespeare explore the feelings and the relationship between Romeo and Friar Lawrence in the passage below?

Friar L: If ere thou wast thyself, and these woes thine,
<u>Thou and these woes were all for Rosaline.</u>
<u>And art thou chang'd?</u> Pronounce this sentence then:
Women may fall when there's no strength in men.
Romeo: Thou chid'st me oft for loving Rosaline.
Friar L: For <u>doting</u>, not for <u>loving</u>, <u>pupil mine</u>.
Romeo: And bad'st me bury love.
Friar L: <u>Not in a grave</u>
To lay one in, another out to have.
Romeo: I pray thee <u>chide me not</u>, her I love now
Doth grace for grace and love for love allow.
The other did not so.
Friar L: <u>O, she knew well</u>
Thy love did <u>read by rote</u> that could not spell.
But <u>come</u> young waverer, <u>come, go with me,</u>
In one respect I'll thy assistant be.
For this alliance may so happy prove
To turn your households' <u>rancour to pure love.</u>

"Rosaline" / "mine" — their lines <u>rhyme</u> with each other, suggesting <u>close relationship</u>.

<u>Poetic technique</u> — The Friar <u>finishes</u> Romeo's lines twice, which highlights his <u>authority</u>.

Here's how you could **Plan** your **Answer** for **Part A...**

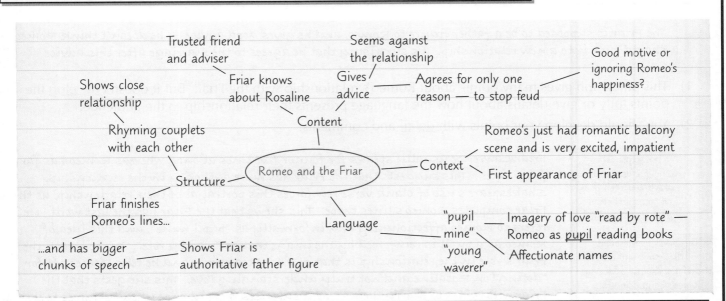

Trusted friend and adviser

Seems against the relationship

Good motive or ignoring Romeo's happiness?

Shows close relationship

Friar knows about Rosaline

Gives advice

Agrees for only one reason — to stop feud

Rhyming couplets with each other

Content

Romeo's just had romantic balcony scene and is very excited, impatient

Romeo and the Friar — Context — First appearance of Friar

Structure

Friar finishes Romeo's lines...

Language

"pupil mine"

Imagery of love "read by rote" — Romeo as <u>pupil</u> reading books

...and has bigger chunks of speech

Shows Friar is authoritative father figure

"young waverer"

Affectionate names

What do examiners eat? Why, egg-sam-wiches of course...

The most important thing to remember is DON'T PANIC. Take a deep breath, read the questions, pick a good 'un, write a plan... take another deep breath... and start writing. Leave 5 minutes at the end to check your answer too.

Worked Answer

These pages will show you how to write a really impressive answer for part A, focusing entirely on the extract given in the exam question. You'll need exactly the same skills to answer part B — the only difference is that for part B you get to choose which part of the play you write about.

Use your **Introduction** *to get off to a* **Good Start**

These pages are all about how to word your sentences to impress the examiner, so we haven't included everything from the plan on page 59.

You might start with something like...

> In this extract, Romeo is asking Friar Lawrence to marry him and Juliet. Their relationship seems close and affectionate. The Friar offers help and advice, whilst Romeo is completely honest about his emotions. They discuss feelings of love.

1) This intro is <u>okay</u>. It describes the relationship and looks at what feelings are shown in the extract.
2) Use the <u>key words</u> from the question to give your essay <u>focus</u>, and to show the examiner you're on <u>track</u> and that you're thinking about the question from the start.
3) But there's still room for <u>improvement</u> — here's a better introduction...

This shows that you're not just describing the relationship, but also focusing on how Shakespeare intended to portray the relationship.

> In this extract, Romeo is asking Friar Lawrence to marry him and Juliet. Shakespeare structures this extract to show the audience that the Friar and Romeo have a close relationship, but also that the Friar takes the fatherly role of judging Romeo and giving advice, whilst Romeo listens and objects. Their dialogue mostly focuses on the change in Romeo's affections, which allows Shakespeare to contrast their different feelings about love and relationships.

This shows a much more detailed understanding of what their relationship is and how they feel.

Develop each point with **Detailed Comments** *and* **Quotes**

> The Friar is supposed to be a father figure to Romeo, and he gives good advice — he doesn't think Romeo should rush into a new relationship. It's surprising that he agrees to the marriage after this advice.

1) This paragraph gives many <u>points</u> about Romeo's relationship with the Friar. But it doesn't <u>develop</u> the points <u>fully</u> or give details about how the language presents their relationship to the audience.
2) You should develop your points with <u>detail</u> and comments:

This explains a technique used in the extract, and then goes on to comment on what that suggests.

This develops the point about the Friar's authority in the relationship by exploring Romeo's contrasting role.

> Friar Lawrence usually speaks for four or five lines at once, whereas Romeo has far fewer lines. This suggests that the Friar has more authority in the relationship. Shakespeare's use of blank verse reinforces this portrayal of their relationship, as the Friar completes Romeo's lines twice. This shows that the Friar has the last word. He refers to Romeo affectionately and informally as "pupil mine", and this idea of Romeo as a pupil is reinforced by the image that he "read by rote". By contrast, the Friar's role in the relationship is that of a wise teacher — and he tells Romeo off for "doting" on Rosaline and not truly understanding love. This suggests that the Friar will refuse to marry them — so it surprises the audience when he agrees to it.

Referring back to the question keeps your answer focused.

Worked Answer

You need to make a *Variety* of *Points*

After you've explained why the audience might expect the Friar to oppose the marriage, you could say this:

> The Friar agrees to marry them for only "one respect" — because it will turn the "rancour to pure love". He wants to end the violence in Verona, and doesn't care that a risky, rushed marriage might be bad for Romeo.

1) This paragraph <u>introduces</u> the idea that the Friar's relationship with Romeo is <u>unreliable</u>.
2) However, you can improve it by discussing <u>how</u> their flawed relationship relates to the <u>themes</u> of the play:

Talking about themes and ideas shows the examiner you're aware of how the extract fits into the play as a whole.

> The Friar thinks their marriage will turn the "rancour to pure love". The reference to the feud reminds the audience of the strength of the violence and hatred in Verona. It affects everything, even decisions about marriage. The feud also affects Romeo's relationship with the Friar, as I think the Friar's motives for marrying them show that he betrays Romeo. They're supposed to have a trusting relationship, but the Friar allows Romeo to do something very dangerous in the hope that it will end the fighting.

Don't forget to explain how your points link to the exam question.

3) Don't forget to focus on characterisation — don't treat the characters as real people.

Mentioning Shakespeare's techniques shows you're aware that the Friar is a fictional character, and you're discussing how he has been portrayed through language and other dramatic devices.

> Shakespeare develops the Friar's character by contrasting what the Friar says and what he does. In this extract the Friar says Romeo is too quick "another out to have", and his emotions have "no strength" because they change too quickly. This makes it sound as if he doubts Romeo's love for Juliet. But then he agrees to marry them. This shows the Friar doesn't listen to his own advice, and makes him seem foolish.

Finish your essay in *Style*

You could say:

> In conclusion, this passage shows that Romeo and the Friar have a pupil/teacher relationship. Romeo trusts the Friar and goes to him for advice. The Friar criticises Romeo but also helps him and tells him what to do.

1) This conclusion is okay but it doesn't summarise <u>how</u> Shakespeare explores the relationship.
2) So to make it really <u>impressive</u> you could say something like...

> At first this extract appears to be a wise Friar affectionately interacting with his headstrong pupil. The fact that the Friar's speech dominates their conversation highlights the fact that he is the authority figure, which develops the idea that they have a pupil/teacher relationship. But in my opinion, this also makes the Friar seem arrogant, and his questionable actions contrast with his wise advice to reveal a lack of wisdom. Therefore, although the affectionate atmosphere of the scene is convincing, Shakespeare's portrayal of the relationship also suggests that the Friar isn't as trustworthy or wise as Romeo thinks.

This shows that you've considered two ways of interpreting the relationship and are expressing a personal opinion about which interpretation is better.

Make your last sentence really stand out — it's your last opportunity to impress the examiner.

Why do alligators write good essays — because their quotes are snappy...

It seems like there's a lot to remember on these two pages, but there's not really. To summarise — write a good intro and conclusion, make a good range of points (one per paragraph) and put your most important point in paragraph one. Easy.

Sample Exam — Planning Part B

Phew, now that's over and it's time for a lovely cup of t... oh wait. Fiddlesticks. There's still Part B to answer.

Decide **Which Bit** of the play to **Write** about

For Part B you need to show the examiner the <u>same</u> essay-writing skills as on <u>pages 60-61</u>.
The <u>tricky</u> bit is <u>planning</u> it — you have to <u>choose</u> the passage, so make sure it's a <u>good one</u>.

1) Read the question <u>closely</u> and underline the <u>important</u> bits.

> **Q1 b)** How does Shakespeare present <u>different aspects</u> of Romeo
> and the Friar's <u>relationship</u> in <u>another part</u> of the play?

2) Think of all the bits in the play that would be <u>relevant</u>. For example, the only other parts of the play that present Romeo's <u>relationship</u> with the Friar are:
<u>Act 2, Scene 6</u> (just before he marries them) and <u>Act 3, Scene 3</u> (when Romeo's just killed Tybalt).

3) Have a <u>quick look</u> at the scenes you could write about and pick the one you feel <u>best fits</u> the question — here are some <u>important points</u> to think about:

- Don't choose a <u>really long</u> passage as you won't be able to cover it in enough <u>detail</u>, but it shouldn't be <u>too short</u> either. Just make sure the passage has enough in it for you to write about.

- Make sure the passage can be linked to the <u>themes</u> and <u>ideas</u> of the play.

- The passage should also have interesting bits of <u>structure</u> or <u>language</u>. You'll have a copy of the text in the exam, so there's no excuse not to include some <u>close analysis</u> of the language.

Here's how you could **Plan** your **Answer** for **Part B**

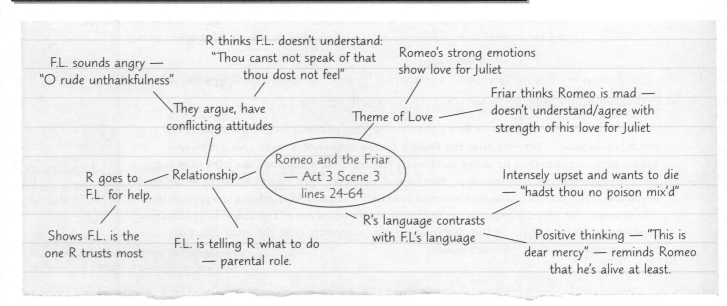

Don't stress about Part B — you might break out in hives...

Keep an eye on the clock, because it's very easy to fritter away precious exam minutes answering Part A perfectly, and neglect Part B. But remember they're worth equal marks — so they need an equal amount of writing time.

Section Six — Assessment Advice

Controlled Assessment Advice

For Controlled Assessments you'll have much more time to prepare your answer — which means you've got no excuse for writing a badly structured essay. Remember these handy hints to make sure it's a bobby dazzler.

Give **Details**, **Opinions**, and cover the **Four Key Areas**

1) It's better to write <u>a few detailed points</u> than to cover lots of <u>different</u> points and not <u>develop</u> any of them.

2) Show that you've got your <u>own opinions</u> — but <u>back up</u> your opinions with evidence from the text.

3) Finally, make sure you have something to say about these <u>four key</u> areas:

- <u>Language</u> — look at Shakespeare's choice of <u>words</u>, use of <u>imagery</u> and <u>punctuation</u>.
- <u>Structure</u> — talk about the play as a <u>whole</u>, and how <u>particular bits</u> fit into the <u>plot</u> or develop <u>themes</u>.
- <u>The Effect on the Audience</u> — <u>explain how</u> Shakespeare intended his <u>techniques</u> to affect the audience.
- <u>Social and Cultural Context</u> — talk about cultural aspects such as <u>courtly love</u> or the position of <u>women</u>.

4) If you're doing <u>AQA English Literature</u>, you might have to <u>compare</u> the play with <u>another</u> text. These four key areas will still be <u>important</u> — compare the language, structure, audience and context of the two texts.

Here's an **Example Controlled Assessment** task

The <u>exam board</u> will set questions for your <u>Controlled Assessment</u> based on themes and ideas, characterisation and voice. This is the sort of question you might have to answer, with a <u>few points</u> you could make:

> **Task 1**   Examine the methods Shakespeare uses to dramatise love and romance in *Romeo and Juliet*.
>
> - <u>Language</u> — <u>Contrast</u> in Romeo's <u>clichéd</u> language and Juliet's more <u>realistic</u> language reveals different views on love. <u>Sonnet</u> forms in their conversations show how in love they are.
> - <u>Structure</u> — Their love is <u>rushed</u> and <u>passionate</u> in the first half of the play, but grows darker and more <u>desperate</u> in the second half.
> - <u>The Effect on the Audience</u> — Shakespeare adds <u>contrast</u> with the Nurse and Mercutio's coarse attitudes to <u>sexual love</u>, to remind the audience how beautiful and romantic Romeo and Juliet's love is.
> - <u>Cultural Context</u> — Romeo's initial views on love are typical of the <u>courtly love</u> tradition.

Use **Quotes** to **Support** your **Ideas**

Remember where to find the key quotes and scenes for your topic, so you don't waste time flicking pages.

1) You're allowed to have a <u>clean copy</u> of the text — so you can include plenty of <u>quotes</u> without having to remember all of them.

2) Don't just use words from the play to prove what <u>happens</u> in the <u>plot</u>.
> The Friar knows Romeo cried a lot for Rosaline: "a deal of brine / Hath wash'd thy sallow cheeks".

3) Instead, it's much better to use quotes as <u>evidence</u> to back up a <u>point</u> you're making.

4) Also, it makes the essay structure <u>clearer</u> and <u>smoother</u> if most quotes are <u>embedded</u> in your sentences.
> The Friar knows that many tears have "wash'd thy sallow cheeks", which shows that Romeo confided in the Friar about his feelings.

WonderQuotes — Now with extra underwiring for better support

When it comes to Controlled Assessment, it's best to float like a boy scout and sting like an elephant — be prepared and never forget. Throw some well-chosen quotes into the mix and you're laughing like Mercutio at clown college.

Index

Index

Index

The Characters in 'Romeo and Juliet'

Phew! You should be an expert on *Romeo and Juliet* by now. But if you want a bit of light relief and a quick recap of what happens in the play, sit yourself down and read through *Romeo and Juliet — The Cartoon...*

The Montagues

Romeo

Montague and
Lady Montague

The Capulets

Juliet

Capulet and
Lady Capulet

Benvolio

Tybalt

Other Characters

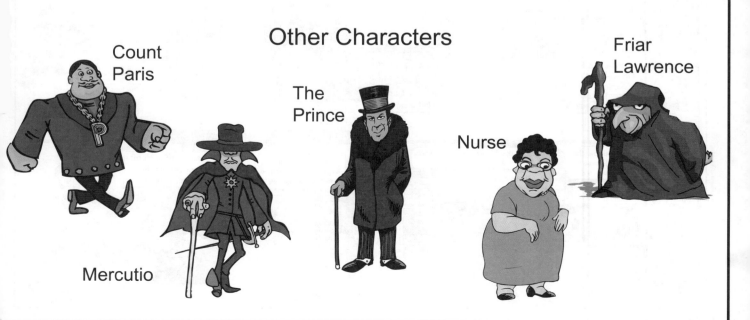

Count
Paris

The
Prince

Friar
Lawrence

Nurse

Mercutio

William Shakespeare's 'Romeo and Juliet'